Clip Notes

for church bulletins

Volume **2** Compiled & edited
by David Philippart

LTP

LITURGY
TRAINING
PUBLICATIONS

CLIPNOTES FOR CHURCH BULLETINS,
VOLUME 2 © 2002 Archdiocese
of Chicago: Liturgy Training
Publications, 1800 North Hermitage
Avenue, Chicago IL 60622-1101;
1-800-933-1800; fax 1-800-933-
7094; orders@ltp.org; www.ltp.org.
All rights reserved.

Visit our website at www.ltp.org.

This book was edited by David
Philippart. Kris Fankhouser was the
production editor. Initial design
by M. Urgo, final design by Anna
Manhart. Karen Mitchell set the
type in Helvetica and Usherwood. It
was printed and bound by Webcom
Limited in Toronto, Canada.

Library of Congress Control
Number: 2002141228

ISBN 1-56854-275-5

NOTES2

Table of Contents

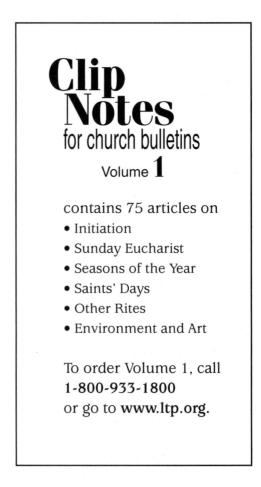

How To Use This Book

Here are 75 articles on various aspects of the liturgy. Grouped into categories for convenience, the articles are not necessarily a comprehensive curriculum on the topic.

You may use these articles in a variety of ways. You might run a topical series of articles four or five weeks in a row as the need arises. Or you might decide to use single articles here and there. Sunday by Sunday through the year, you simply may chose to include one article that seems timely. The "Suggested Schedule Sunday by Sunday" at the end of the book gives you advice how to use one article a week beginning with the First Sunday of Advent in any given year. In some weeks, there are two or three articles to choose from. But these are just suggestions.

The "Record of Use Chart" at the back of the book helps you to keep track of how the articles are used. This will help you remember if you already put a particular article in the Sunday bulletin or in the school or religious education newsletter, for example.

No page numbers appear on the actual article. Article numbers are found on the opposite blank page. Nothing else is placed on the back of the article to make it as easy to copy as possible. There are four ways to reproduce these articles: 1. Photocopy a page directly. 2. Scan the article and its art directly from the book using your scanner. 3. Use the supplied CD-ROM to transfer text and art into your word processing or page makeup program. 4. Use the Acrobat Portable Document File (also on the CD-ROM) for an exact electronic reproduction of a page. No matter how you reproduce this, the copyright notice must always appear as written with the text and art.

You are free to copy the text and art in this book for your parish, school or institution provided that you are not selling the publication in which it appears, or distributing the publication in connection with a program or event for which you are charging a fee. If you are selling the publication, or distributing the publication in connection with a program or event for which you are charging a fee, you must write for permission. In your letter, state exactly which articles and art you wish to copy, how many copies you will make and what you will charge per copy. Please allow at least one month for a reply. There may be a fee. Write to:

Reprint Permission
Liturgy Training Publications
1800 North Hermitage Avenue
Chicago IL 60622-1101

You may send a fax to 773-486-7094. We would be happy to hear your suggestions about topics for subsequent volumes of Clip Notes. Write to or fax:

The Editor of Clip Notes
Liturgy Training Publications
1800 North Hermitage Avenue
Chicago IL 60622-1101

More art is available in Liturgy Training Publications' series of clip-art books by Steve Erspamer: *Clip Art for Year A, Clip Art for Year B* and *Clip Art for Year C.* (These are also available on disk.) Suzanne Novak's *Clip Art for Parish Life* also has art designed especially for bulletins and newsletters. To order, call: 1-800-933-1800, or send an e-mail message to *orders@ltp.org* or go online to *www.ltp.org.* One new bulletin article and illustration is published in each issue of the magazine Rite, published eight times a year. To subscribe, call: 1-800-933-1800.

The Whole Church Celebrates with You

We're getting married!" With these few, simple words, an engaged couple announces the most important decision of their lives. This decision affects not only the couple, but also their families and friends. No longer is John just "our son," "our nephew" or "my college buddy;" no longer is Mary just "my daughter," "our cousin" or "my friend from work." Now they are also partners who have agreed to pledge their lives to each other and form a new family.

desires so as to live for each other and their children. Their marriage reflects Christ's relationship with the church and creates a new family within the community of the church.

A church wedding touches the couple, their families and friends in an especially intimate way, but it also pertains to the local parish and to the larger church. This is what the bishops at the Second Vatican Council meant when they said, "Liturgical services are not private functions but are

As they gather around John and Mary at the wedding, these family members and friends celebrate these changes in relationships.

When a wedding is celebrated in church, there is another level of relationship beyond family and friends, and that involves God and the church. In their exchange of vows, the couple offers a visible sign of God's presence and love. It is an act of worship that takes place in the midst of a Christian community. In living out their vows, husband and wife share in Christ's paschal mystery by dying to their own

celebrations of the Church which is 'the sacrament of unity'" (*Constitution on the Sacred Liturgy,* 26). Catholic weddings are parish liturgies and, as such, are often announced in the parish bulletin. Weddings may even be celebrated within a parish Sunday Mass. While one may need an invitation to attend the reception, the wedding liturgy is a celebration of the whole church and is open to all parishioners.

Q&A: Always at Mass?

Is the wedding always a Mass?

The church's *Rite of Marriage,* published in 1969 as part of the liturgical reforms following the Second Vatican Council (1962–1965), actually provides three forms for a Catholic wedding liturgy. "The Rite for Celebrating Marriage During Mass" is normally used when two Catholics marry. "The Rite for Celebrating Marriage Outside Mass" is used when a Catholic marries a baptized person from another Christian church. "The Rite for Celebrating Marriage Between a Catholic and an Unbaptized Person" is used when a Catholic marries someone who is not a baptized Christian, including a catechumen.

In the first form, the wedding (the rite of marriage) is celebrated within Mass—between the liturgy of the word and the liturgy of the eucharist. In the second and third forms, the marriage rite is celebrated after the liturgy of the word, which ends with a concluding rite instead of being followed with the liturgy of the eucharist. Each of these forms is equally valid and holy.

A wedding is a holy celebration. Whenever a Catholic marries a baptized person, whether that person is Catholic or from another Christian church, the marriage is considered a sacrament. (When a Catholic marries someone who is not baptized, the marriage is recognized and blessed by the church, but it is not by definition a sacrament because sacramental marriage involves a covenant between two baptized people.) The different forms of celebration are an attempt to respect the consciences of all involved and to enable a celebration in which all can participate.

Why might it be a good idea to celebrate one of the two forms of the wedding liturgy that do not include Mass? Even if only one partner is Catholic, shouldn't she or he "receive communion" on the wedding day? It would, of course, be good for the couple to be able to share in the eucharist after exchanging their vows. But if both bride and groom cannot (and this also may mean that many friends and family members of either bride or groom cannot), it is often better not to celebrate the eucharist. The eucharist is our ultimate sacrament of unity—of communion. To celebrate the eucharist in a situation where a large number of those present cannot share in it, especially where the bride or the groom is noticeably unable to share in it, runs the risk of turning this very sacrament of communion into a sign of something that divides instead of unites us. This is why the church gives us three forms with which to celebrate marriage.

3

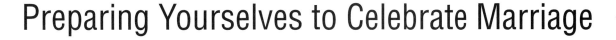

Preparing Yourselves to Celebrate Marriage

The months before a wedding are usually a time of intense planning for the "big day." Here are three things not to overlook in preparing for a Catholic wedding:

1.) In the Roman Catholic Church, the couple is the minister of the sacrament of marriage. The bride and groom exchange vows to each other. The priest or deacon serves as the church's chief witness; he does not "pronounce them husband and wife." Other roles in a Catholic wedding include two additional witnesses (the "best man" and "maid of honor"), lectors to proclaim the scripture readings and intercessions, music ministers to lead the assembly's singing, and, if the wedding takes place within Mass, additional ministers of communion (as needed).

2.) Some things are essential for a Catholic wedding; others are not. Essential things include the scripture readings, homily, statement of intentions ("Have you come here freely and without reservation. . . ?"), consent or exchange of vows, and nuptial blessing. Things that are not essential include seating guests of the bride and guests of the groom on separate sides of the aisle, keeping the bride and groom apart before the wedding, unrolling a white aisle runner before the entrance procession, lighting a unity or wedding candle, and placing flowers before a statue of Mary.

3.) There are no spectators at a Catholic wedding. The bishops at the Second Vatican Council made "full, conscious, and active participation" by all worshippers "the aim to be considered before all else" in liturgy (*Constitution on the Sacred Liturgy,* 14). Just as at Sunday Mass, certain individuals fulfill various ministries within the wedding liturgy, but the entire assembly of worshippers celebrates the liturgy. When you go to a wedding, listen attentively to the scriptures the couple has chosen, sing the music they have selected, respond to the prayers in a strong voice. The enthusiastic participation of the entire assembly of worshippers is the best gift anyone can give to the couple on their "big day."

Wedding Traditions

Have you ever heard the old wedding rhyme that suggests that the bride should carry "something old, something new, something borrowed, something blue?" Most weddings involve some combination of old and new as couples try to reflect their continuity with the weddings that have gone before theirs as well as what is unique in their marriage. Those who favor what they think of as the old often speak of their wedding as "traditional," while those who favor what they consider to be new often

consists of social customs from another era that no longer correspond to the church's (or even a modern man's or woman's) understanding of marriage. For example, at one time people believed that it was "bad luck" for the groom to see the bride before the ceremony began. The *Catechism of the Catholic Church* refers to such superstitions as a "perverse excess of religion" and a "deviation of religious feeling" (#2110–2111). The custom whereby the bride's father "gives the bride away" to the groom at the

refer to theirs as "contemporary." More often than not, these terms simply imply a particular style.

For Catholics, weddings are both traditional and contemporary in the best sense of these terms. Each Catholic wedding is traditional because it hands on and enfleshes the church's faith concerning the sacrament of marriage. (The root of the Latin word *traditio* literally means "to hand down" or "to hand over.") Each Catholic wedding is contemporary because it makes present *here* and *now* in *this unique marriage,* God's love for the couple and Christ's relationship with the church.

Much of what is popularly considered "traditional" at weddings actually

head of the aisle reflects a time when marriages were arranged between the groom and the bride's father, and in some cases, the woman was seen as property to be given and received. Today, the church and society both emphasize marriage as a mutual decision by equal and free partners.

Wedding customs that no longer reflect reality or faith are meaningless. Authentic wedding traditions "hand down" the church's ageless faith in ways that respect the current social reality of marriage and the contemporary Christian understanding of marriage.

Here Comes the Bride . . . and the Groom . . . and Their Parents!

If television and the movies are to be believed, every North American wedding (at least among English-speaking people) begins with the tune popularly known as *Here Comes the Bride.* As all eyes turn to gaze admiringly on the bride walking down the aisle, the groom slips unnoticed to his place at the head of the aisle. In reality, this stereotype is beginning to break down.

Here Comes the Bride, which is actually the *Bridal Chorus* from Wagner's opera *Lohengrin,* has been eclipsed in popularity by other processionals such as Purcell's *Trumpet Tune* and Clarke's *Trumpet Voluntary.* The major limitation of *Here Comes the Bride* is its association with just the bride, whereas the Roman Catholic *Rite of Marriage* addresses bride *and* groom as equal partners who together undertake the covenant of marriage. The entrance procession as envisioned by the church includes both bride and groom who "may be escorted by at least their parents and the two witnesses" (*Rite of Marriage,* 20). During the wedding liturgy, the bride and groom together serve as the minister of the sacrament of marriage. Even apart from the liturgy, many of the wedding preparations that had been the domain of the bride and her mother are increasingly being shared by the groom.

The participation of the groom in the entrance procession does not eliminate the bride's father from his place in the procession, just as the involvement of the groom in preparations for the wedding does not mean that the couple won't need the assistance of the bride's mother. The bride's parents, and the groom's parents as well, have played an important role in bringing their son or daughter to this point in life. By including both sets of parents in the entrance procession, the wedding liturgy honors the families that have shaped the bride and groom as they come together to establish a new family.

6

Q&A: Who Marches up the Aisle?

The recommended procedure that is described in the current *Rite of Marriage* is that the bride, accompanied by her parents, and the groom, accompanied by his parents, join in the entrance procession with the other ministers of the wedding celebration. The problem (at least in the United States) is that, in general, people have been ignoring the rubrics regarding the entrance procession found in the *Rite of Marriage* and continuing a older custom that has pre-Christian roots.

The current rite explains "If there is a procession to the altar, the ministers go first, followed by the priest, and then the bride and bridegroom. According to local custom, they may be escorted by at least their parents and the two witnesses. Meanwhile, the entrance song is sung" (#20). The Roman rite is sensitive to local custom, but it provides a model which should be seen as presenting certain values. In my mind, some of the values enshrined here are (1) the equality of the spouses (both bride and groom enter together), (2) the equality of both parents (both mother and father join both spouses) and (3) an integration of the "bridal" procession into the traditional entrance procession of the Mass.

There is little to be said in favor of the "traditional" bridal entrance. It can be rightly criticized for perpetuating the image that the bride is the "property" of her father, who alone has the right to "give her away" to another man (the groom). Using such an image is a poor way to start a marriage and not an ideal practice to incorporate into a contemporary Catholic liturgy, which celebrates the equality of all people before God.

From a ritual point of view, such a bridal entrance detracts from the structure and flow of the opening rites. Our tradition is to be begin with the entrance procession of the ministers (if not the whole assembly), with all giving voice to a common hymn and thus being united into the body of Christ. To stand and watch a parade is foreign to our sense of liturgy. And since the bride and the groom are the principal ministers of the sacrament of marriage, why not have them enter as ministers of the liturgy usually do?

Even though Hollywood movies and TV shows perpetuate the "traditional" bridal entrance procession, I think such a practice should be relegated to museums and the procession suggested by the ritual become the standard practice in contemporary worship celebrations in Catholic churches.

Wedding Music

Planning a wedding is exciting. Couples are faced with many choices and receive a lot of advice from well meaning family and friends. When planning music for a wedding celebration, it seems that everyone has a well intentioned opinion. Couples also pick up ideas from the music played at friends' weddings and the weddings they see on television or in movies. Not all of these suggestions or selections are appropriate for the celebration of the sacrament of marriage.

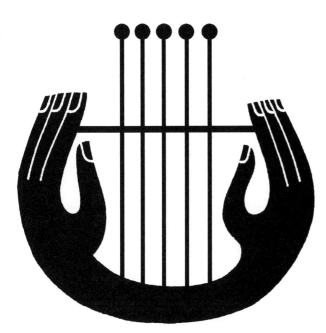

Music is an integral part of any liturgy. It is not something extra, but a part of the organic structure of the liturgy. In the words of the United States Bishops' Committee on the Liturgy, "Great care should be taken, especially at marriages, that all the people are involved at the important moments of the celebration, that the same general principles of planning worship and judging music are employed as at other liturgies, and, above all, that the liturgy is a prayer for all present, not a theatrical production" (*Music in Catholic Worship,* 82).

The parish music director is a valuable resource for couples planning their wedding liturgy. He or she can provide names of trained instrumentalists and cantors who would be available to lead the music for the wedding. The music director also has a varied list of musical repertoire that is familiar to the parish and contains texts that are appropriate for the liturgical and sacramental action of a wedding. Such texts don't reduce marriage to sweet sentimental thoughts or focus exclusively on the bride and groom. Rather, they speak of the love of God, the love for God, the love God has for this couple and the church, and the covenant that the couple is establishing in marriage. Once your wedding date is set, contact the parish music director!

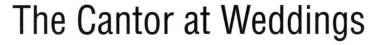

The Cantor at Weddings

The liturgy of marriage is a celebration of the entire community. It calls for family members, friends and members of the parish community to gather around the couple not as spectators, but as active participants in a liturgy.

A good cantor (the word comes from the Latin and means "song leader") inspires participation during the wedding liturgy. As a minister of hospitality, the cantor can take

a few minutes before the procession to welcome the arriving guests and lead a short rehearsal of unfamiliar music, if necessary. In a friendly and inviting manner, the cantor in one parish explains, "It is our parish's custom to sing the liturgy. Since we come from different places, let us take a moment as we begin to rehearse the responsorial psalm." This simple act of hospitality lets the assembly know that there is an expectation that all will participate in the singing.

The cantor is also usually the psalmist for the liturgy, proclaiming the verses of the responsorial psalm during the liturgy of the word and leading the assembly in singing the refrain. A soloist should never replace the cantor or sing in place of the assembly. The cantor leads the assembly in its sung prayer, and a soloist performs for an audience.

Many people are reticent to sing at weddings. Sometimes, it's because they are not Catholic or because they have not been to church in a while. Often, they've just gotten used to *listening* to music at weddings rather than *taking part* in the singing. Experience has shown that assemblies feel more confident singing acclamations, hymns and songs when led by a cantor from the front of the church. If your parish doesn't automatically provide one, your parish music director can help you find a competent cantor to minister at your wedding. An assembly joined together in sung prayer, praise and blessing is a wonderful gift to give a couple beginning their lives together!

Preparing Your Wedding Liturgy

Many engaged couples schedule their weddings a year or more in advance. Some reception facilities require at least this much advance notice, and the myriad details involved in wedding planning can easily occupy a couple for the better part of a year! For a couple planning to marry in the church, a major focus during this time is their preparation for the sacrament of marriage. Using a variety of formats, a parish's or diocese's marriage preparation

program help couples prepare for the life-long covenant they will establish at their wedding. The couples' reflections on their faith and the church's faith concerning marriage are an important starting point for their preparations for the wedding liturgy.

The church's *Rite of Marriage* presents the couple as the minister of the sacrament of marriage and invites their participation in the preparation of the wedding liturgy. In conjunction with the priest or deacon who will preside at the wedding, the couple chooses among several options for the various prayer texts and scripture readings that will be proclaimed at the wedding liturgy. With the parish music director, the couple chooses hymns, acclamations, a responsorial psalm and instrumental music. Individuals need to be asked to serve as ushers, lectors and ministers of the eucharist. Most parishes provide couples with a book to guide them through these choices.

Like the other aspects of a wedding, the wedding liturgy is more apt to be free of anxiety and open to genuine celebration if it has been prepared well in advance of the wedding day. No one is served well by leaving decisions and details to the last minute. By preparing the wedding liturgy *together,* the couple has a wonderful opportunity to share their faith with each other, to explore the church's faith concerning marriage in the scriptures, to discover the ways in which their families celebrated special events, and to practice the kind of selfless concern for each other that will nurture and sustain the life-long covenant of marriage.

Wedding Customs

Some things are common to all Catholic weddings: scripture readings, declaration of freedom to marry, exchange of vows, nuptial blessing. Beyond these "basics," many weddings include customs that are not required by the church's *Rite of Marriage,* but that are significant within a particular ethnic group or local community.

Ethnic Customs: In many Eastern rites, crowns are placed on the heads of the bride and groom as a symbol their baptismal inheritance of the kingdom of God. In some Filipino weddings, the couple offers a sign of respect toward their parents, godparents and elders. Recalling a ceremony that originated in the days of slavery, some African-American couples jump over a broom to symbolize their step into matrimony and the beginnings of their homemaking. Mexican wedding customs include the exchange of arras, coins which represent the couple's promise to provide and use wisely what will be necessary to sustain their home, and the placing of a lazo or yoke (often a double-looped rosary) across the shoulders of the couple as a symbol of the marriage union.

Other Customs: Some couples place flowers before a statue or image of Mary as they invoke Mary's selfless love as a model for their marriage. Some light a candle from two smaller candles, indicating that the new family that is established in this wedding is formed from two existing families. Reflecting their role as the minister of the sacrament of marriage, some couples greet arriving guests at the doors of the church, introducing the guests to their parents and thanking them for their presence at the wedding. In another emerging custom, the couple presents a large basket of food for a local food pantry or soup kitchen along with the bread and wine for the Mass.

Customs such as these are at their best when they support, but not overshadow, the primary elements of the wedding liturgy. To be authentic, they should reflect the couple's faith and the faith of the church concerning marriage, not merely imitate something done at another wedding.

Giving a Blessing

There are occasions in our human experience that suddenly touch us and we grope for words to mark the moment: A friend lies gravely ill, a family member embarks on a journey, a child is afraid of the dark and cannot sleep, a daughter reaches menarche, a relative announces a wonderful promotion, a spouse retires from a long career. . . .

Perhaps the words we are searching for and the gesture that would express our hope for that person could take the form of a blessing. The Celts have along tradition of bestowing blessings. Bestowing a blessing is a gentle gift. You can put your hands on the head or shoulders of the other and say a simple prayer. Mention your hope for that person and ask for the necessary graces. If you saved blessed water from the Easter Vigil and have it stored away in a bottle for just such occasions, use some in a sprinkling rite. It reminds us of our baptism and affirms our identity and purpose.

We can feel free to devise a blessing with our own words or we can learn some blessings from the Celts:

Grace upwards over thee,
Grace downwards over thee,
Grace of graces without gainsaying,
Grace of Father and of Lord.
The joy of God be in thy face,
Joy to all who see thee;
The circling of God be keeping thee,
Angels of God shielding thee.
God bless to you this day,
God bless to you this night;
Bless, O bless, Thou God of grace,
Each day and hour of your life;
Bless, O bless, Thou God of grace,
Each day and hour of your life.

Remembering the Dead

Summer's abundance and sun-drenched extroversion is finally over. The harvest has been gathered indoors. The garden's excess has been turned under the earth. Autumn would look like death if we didn't know nature's cyclic patterns. Our religious feasts coincide with nature. In a few weeks we will remember the saints and souls of our forbears who have died. As the harvest has been gathered into barns, these souls have been gathered as a heavenly harvest. And it is right that we remember them as part of the communion of saints. In a corner of the house on a mantel or small table, begin to collect up photographs of people who have been significant in your life and who are now gone. During November, light a votive lamp before their pictures and take turns telling their stories and remembering what you know or have heard about them. Tell of their strengths and tell of their weaknesses. Mention a trait that you think you may have inherited from one or another relative and then mention a talent that you would like to develop in yourself. Conclude your remembrance with a prayer that these souls may sleep the sleep of peace. At the eucharist, mention them silently by name as we remember all those who have gone before us.

Gift Giving

Gift-giving at Christmas is meant to be an expression of our joy and exuberance over the gift of God to us: Jesus. The name "Emanuel" means God-with-us and every created thing has something of God in it. Julian of Norwich said it this way: "God is everything that is good. And the goodness in things is God." Certainly the very holiness of gift-giving also makes it a gesture vulnerable to all that is unholy! How many resentments do we harbor around the gifts we gave, received, or failed to receive? And how vulnerable we are to the tempest the world whips up so that we might spend our money—rather than our time or creativity?

Cut back your gift-giving to a manageable size. Infuse your gift preparations with joy and imagination. Consider making your gifts. To make gifts for one another allows our creativity to join in the Creator's. Children need parental help in preparing their presents for the family. Give each child an evening a week with one parent so that they can plan and make their gifts in secret.

Remember there are at least twelve days of Christmas: from December 24 until the feast of the Baptism of the Lord. All the days of Christmas are appropriate for giving and receiving gifts. We don't have to be in a hurry to get it all done by December 24. We can spread out our joy and celebration of the season by spreading out giving of gifts.

14

Lent at Home

Lent means spring. This is a season for a new awakening. It means cleaning out the dust and grime of a long, dark winter. It means the melting of ice and snow and the first, cautious appearance of things sprouting. So it is also in our hearts during this season. Our spirit is invited to a thorough spring house-cleaning. We are given the rags and dust mops and brooms of that spiritual refreshment in the tools called prayer, fasting, and almsgiving. We pray for the good of our souls. We fast for the good of our bodies. We give alms for the good of our sisters and brothers. Notice that these tools are always "for the *good* of" something.

Sloppy habits in our prayer life leave us feeling out of kilter with God in our deepest selves—disconnected and at odds. Get yourself a different translation of the Book of Psalms and wake up your inner ear to a bright, sparkling sound that rattles out a dull language of habit and routine. Memorize your favorite psalm in this new translation and allow it to take root in your soul. (To order a copy, call 1-800-933-1800.)

Fast for the good of your body. That may mean eating with awareness and appreciation rather than nibbling and grazing all day long. It may mean eating meals as a shared experience with family and/or friends. It may mean changing your unhealthy eating habits by changing your diet. It may mean doing without some compulsion you harbor or without a food you take for granted, so that your body feels a difference and appreciates again, in the days of Easter, that which it missed during Lent. And all the cuts of meat you did without, the deserts, the beers, the movies, the sweets, the cigarettes—these can be graphically translated into alms for those who are hungry and would love a bowl of rice, a thick soup, a needed medicine. Fasting wakes up the mind and sharpens our awareness of others and more readily fixes our attention beyond what is merely selfish.

prayer   *fasting*   *almsgiving*

Feasting at Easter

Finally the apex of our spiritual journey has been reached in the resurrection of Jesus. Around this feast every other feast circles. We fill the freshly scrubbed house with spring flowers. We hang bright eggs from budding branches. We bake our tall resurrection breads and Easter cakes. We invite family and friends to find eggs in the garden and to share in a hearty feast. Having carried home the Easter water and the Easter fire from the vigil the night before, we are ready to sprinkle everyone and everything with a douse from our baptismal springs. We take the holy fire to rekindle candles, the hearth, even the pilot lights of water heater and stove! This Easter fire is what warms and what brightens every aspect of our lives. Through these holy signs, the ordinary actions of a hot shower or a warmed soup become extraordinary and imbued with the mystery of the resurrection.

So when you come to the vigil, bring a jar for the water, and a votive candle in glass to bring home the fire.

On Mealtime as Prayer

Eating together as family, with friends or in community is as old a human expression as history can recall. The very word "companion" means "the one you share your bread with." Sharing food is just as nourishing to the soul as eating is nourishing for the body. How is it that in recent years the family meal has suffered such disintegration? All day we graze and nibble and by dinner time, we are no longer hungry. We are so busy, that we cannot cook, or cannot sit together over food and drink to share the events of the day and the issues that burn in our hearts. The average American family eats dinner in about five minutes!

In these Easter days, beyond the meal shared which we call the "last supper," we hear that the risen Jesus shared his bread at the end of a long walk with his grieving disciples on the road to Emmaus. He broke bread with them and "they knew him in the breaking of the bread." Every meal that we share is an occasion to "know him" — to recognize Christ in the heart of the persons with whom we share our meal. We also hear the story of a fish fry that the risen Jesus prepared for his friends after a night of fishing. How concrete. How physical. How human. How loving. Ghosts don't cook for us. But the bodily presence of a risen Lord knows our bodily hungers and provides for us in material ways. To share what we have with another is to "know him." To break bread with a blessing is to help us remember that every meal looks concretely to the meal. And it isn't possible to comprehend the eucharistic meal if we don't understand the sacramentality of the daily meal.

Collect blessings for your table. Offer a variety of words and songs so that your prayers do not become routine or unimaginative. Take time to enjoy your meal and to enjoy one another. If you live alone, invite others in to share your bread.

I saw a stranger today
I put food for him
    in the eating place
And drink in the drinking place.
In the Holy Name of the Trinity
He blessed myself
    and my house
My goods and my family.
And the lark said in her warble
Often, often, often
Goes Christ
    in the stranger's guise
0, oft and oft and oft,
Goes Christ
    in the stranger's guise.
— *An Irish rune of hospitality*

Mass Begins at Home

We refer to our arrival in the church before the celebration as "the gathering rite." Most of us think of it as the moment when we meet and greet our brothers and sisters in Christ early in the liturgy. But we can think of it as a rite that begins much earlier: Even as we arrive on the church grounds and get out of our cars in the parking lot, as we greet and talk with the others about the weather or about which of our children caught the chickenpox—the gathering rite is in motion. Even earlier, roused from our sleep, we have begun to

gather our wits and collect our thoughts and intentions. Hauled from our beds, we have migrated from all directions to form this gathering. For we are hungry to break the bread that is Christ's body and share the cup of our salvation.

The gathering rite is our invitation to hone our awareness of this migration we make on Sunday morning. It gives the chance to make a transition from the sacrament of daily life to the sacrament of our gathered community. We do not want to find ourselves in this migration out of habit or duty—but we want to reach that level of awareness that knows our deepest yearning for an experience of the holy in communion.

Here are some ideas to make the gathering rite a joyful, rich and pleasant experience before you even arrive at the church: Get up an hour earlier and read over the scripture lessons for the day so that you can really hear them at the liturgy. Make special coffee or hot chocolate and bring it around to family members inviting them to this Sunday rising with plenty of time to shower and dress in their Sunday clothes. Allow that the family retains a Sunday silence—no idle chatter—just the peace of silence and a gathering of our inner selves. Play "Sunday music"—to set the tone: chant or some meditative and beautiful religious music from our long heritage. Retain the silence as you walk or drive to church. When you arrive, make a point of greeting and engaging the others you meet. Greet someone you know already and greet and make the acquaintance of someone whom you have never met before. "Where two or three are gathered in my name, there am I in the midst of you."

Keeping Sunday

This is the day the Lord has made, let us rejoice and be glad in it.

Even before you open your eyes in the early mornings don't you think about the day ahead? To wake up to the fact that it is Sunday and a day not like the others in feeling and spirit means that you have a way of celebrating this day; that you know the art of celebrating a feast. You know that Sunday is a day created for our benefit. It means to give us a taste of heaven. But if Sunday is merely a day to make it to church on time, then you may need some ways to make Sunday special.

A special Sunday begins on Friday night. By sundown on Friday, try to have a clean slate. Complete what needs doing—finish off the unpleasant chores. Clean off your desk. Get the grocery shopping done for the weekend so you don't have to shop on Sunday (thereby asking others to serve you in the shops on Sunday). It is important to take time to repair your relationships with the rest of the family.

Use Saturday to ready your home for Sunday. Put the house and yard in order. Wash the car. Change the linens. Cook something special for Sunday's brunch. Bring fresh flowers to brighten the table. Read tomorrow's gospel as a family and talk about it. Put the children to bed with greater attention. Saturday night is a special opportunity for the adults to spend time together repairing and enjoying their relationships.

On Sunday, begin the new week in a special way. Put Sunday music on the stereo. Avoid all unnecessary talk. Go from bedroom to bedroom speaking the ancient monastic greeting: "Let us arise and bless the Lord." Dress in your "Sunday best;" if you've recently bought new clothes, wear them for the first time on a Sunday. Sunday clothes are a metaphor for our baptismal garments. Don't watch TV or read the Sunday papers before eucharist.

At brunch, use a special meal prayer. Then change from your "Sunday best" to clothes for relaxation and play. Resolve to do no unnecessary work. Go to a museum, the park, the beach, the zoo, or the mountains. Play the piano, read a book, go swimming, play ball, read the fat Sunday papers. Family members or friends can take turns planning Sunday's recreation. If there is a special ball game or television program that is truly worth watching, watch it together. Preparing Sunday dinner can be a cooperative undertaking—and Sunday dinner can be one day in the week you can count on everyone being together. It's also a good meal to invite a friend. Use the good table cloth and the good dishes. Whatever you undertake to do on Sunday, do it without haste or anxiety. Sunday is a day meant to restore and refresh us. Sunday is a day to become fully human.

Walking Meditation

There is a Buddhist exercise that teaches us to appreciate the sacramentality of nature and living in the present moment. It is called "walking meditation." It is designed to stop us from hurrying, pacing, dashing, and rushing, when our "steps print anxiety and sorrow on the Earth." In this meditation we walk slowly, alone or with a friend, preferably in a beautiful place. We walk as though we were the happiest person on earth. We walk, not thinking about the past or worrying about the future. We walk, not trying to get from here to there. We stop our minds from darting around. We transform our walking path to a field for meditation — our feet taking every step in full awareness. Breathing and stepping are in harmony. Then we can pray, perhaps, with the poet, Gerard Manly Hopkins:

> The world is charged with the grandeur
>   of God.
> It will flame out, like shining from
>   shook foil:
> It gathers to a greatness, like the ooze
>   of oil . . .
>
> And for all this, nature is never spent;
> There lives the dearest freshness deep
>   down things . . .

More on Walking Meditation

There is a Zen tradition called "walking meditation" which invites us to do exactly what we do all the time: walk! But now we are invited to walk with awareness, slowly, mindfully. Not walking in order to hurry from here to there, but walking for its own sake and to be purely in the present moment, enjoying each step we take. If we transform our daily walks into a meditation, our feet will take each step with awareness. Our breathing and our stepping will be in harmony and our mind will be free to find peace and joy. And to cause peace and joy to flow through us to others. As far back as 1930, Romano Guardini, the great Catholic liturgist, also spoke of the sacramentality of walking: "Walking is the expression of essentially human nobility. The upright carriage of the who masters one's self, who bears one's self along calmly and quietly—that is a human privilege." Walking upright means being a human.

But we are even more than just human. Scripture says that we are the "offspring of God, reborn of God to a new life." Imagine! We should walk as though we remembered that Christ lives in us. His body dwells in our flesh; his blood circulates in our veins. For "they that eat my flesh and drink my blood, abide in me and I in them." Guardini goes on to say "The knowledge of this mystery could find its expression in walking rightly, joyfully, with graceful and firm movement. It could be a profound fulfillment of the command: 'Walk before me and be perfect.'"

We can transform our "daily constitutional" into walking meditation. Breathing and stepping in rhythm. Watching the firm, joyful steps we take. Walking in the faith that Christ is formed in us; that all that we do has become part of Christ's life in us.

Q&A: Godparents

Who may be godparents for our baby's baptism?

Godparents should be both role models and resource persons, individuals who are at ease with the practice of their faith and would normally be considered "active" Catholics. They should be people who are comfortable with answering questions about their personal relation with God as experienced in the Catholic communion, even if they are unsure about all the technicalities. They should be people who are interested in and will continue to support their godchild in the years ahead as they and their godchild develop in their relationships with God and others.

Church law specifies that godparents be at least sixteen years old and themselves have been fully initiated, that is, have received the sacraments of baptism, confirmation and first communion. It is also assumes that godparents have been asked to serve in this role by the individual to be baptized (or, in the case of infants, by the family or, if they do not know anyone, the local pastor). The other requirements stipulate that parents should not be godparents, nor should anyone whose status in the church is questionable.

The role of the godparent is not merely that of patron—it is that of mentor. And so, sometimes emotional conflicts occur in a family when relatives or close friends who are held in esteem are considered as possible godparents, but are technically not qualified either because they are not Catholics or because they are Catholics who do not practice their faith regularly or whose religious status is "problematic"

because of some situation, for example, a civil marriage not blessed by the church.

It is occasionally permitted for a non-Catholic Christian to be associated as a "Christian witness" to a baptism. Though not officially a godparent, such an individual can still function as a role model for someone who is trying to learn about how a person should follow Christ in our troublesome world. In such situations, another person should be designated as the official godparent, someone who fits into the traditional categories.

Most people are aware of the conflicts that can occur between loyalties based on relationships and friendship and the demands of liturgical and religious authenticity. Not every relative or friend is appropriate to serve as godparent, and not every person who is appropriate as a godparent is close enough to serve in that capacity for the family. Balance is not easy to achieve! In special cases, the advice of the local priest or pastoral minister can be very helpful.

Q&A: Confirmation Names

Should I encourage my child to pick a confirmation name?

Our names are used at our baptism and become part of our religious history. For many centuries it was customary only to use the names of saints at baptism, but the baptismal rite now permits other names as long as they are not incompatible with Christian faith and the Rite of Christian Initiation of Adults even provides a rite for a catechumen to receive a "Christian" name before baptism (RCIA, 202). Any discussion of a "confirmation name" must be placed in the context of the relationship of confirmation to baptism.

Confirmation is a "seal" of the faith and grace given in baptism. The current rite of confirmation tries to link the celebration of this sacrament of initiation to baptism and thus, for example, recommends that the "sponsor" for confirmation be, when possible, the baptismal godparent and includes a formal renewal of baptismal promises after the homily. Since the rite contains no specific directive otherwise, it presumes that those to be confirmed will be addressed by the name used at their baptism.

Choosing a separate confirmation name had been a centuries-old custom for those baptized as infants but confirmed later, but this practice emphasizes a separation between the two sacraments that is at variance with our renewed understanding of the relationship of baptism, confirmation, and eucharist as the three sacraments of Christian initiation. And, although popular in many places, in actual fact a "confirmation name" is nowhere mentioned either in the former rite or in the current rite nor is

it mentioned either in the old or new Codes of Canon Law.

Today there may be appropriate and pastoral reasons for someone to choose another patron saint and use this saint's name when being confirmed. This name, freely chosen and reflective of the candidate's devotion to a saint, can be a sign of commitment to living as a Christian in today's world under the patronage of someone they admire. Ideally such a confirmation name would be used in addition to the baptismal name, and not in place of it, and would be a saint to whom the person being confirmed has a particular devotion.

For most individuals, though, using the baptismal name alone can be a powerful reaffirmation of who they are as Christians. Whether a person chooses a special patron and name at confirmation or chooses to honor the name received at baptism should always be considered as really a secondary aspect of the celebration. What is ultimately being celebrated is God's commitment to each baptized Christian through the gift of the Holy Spirit.

Keeping Silence

In the liturgy, we are silent, silent *together*. This is not an individual silence, even though each of us—as best as each of is able—is quiet. This is not a passive silence, even though we try to be as still as we can be. We are silent together, actively quiet, purposely still. We're silent before the liturgy begins, in order to be present to each other and thus find God. God is always present to us; we forget that sometimes, fail to hear God amid our noisy living. So before we wrestle with God in our rites, we are silent: Be still, and know that I am God.

We are silent at the words "Let us pray." These words begin the opening prayer and prayer after communion at Mass, as well as the prayers after the psalms at morning and evening prayer. At this invitation, we pray and we pray hard and we pray hard together, so that when the priest speaks, all of our prayers are drawn to those words like metal shavings to a magnet. One voice breaks the silence with words of prayer, and one mighty voice, spoken from all of our throats, seals that prayer: "Amen!"

We are silent after readings of scripture and after the homily. How else can God speak to us? How else are we to hear the divine voice, not only echoing from long ago in ancient words brought back to life, but speaking now, in this time, in the quiet that we provide here? After the readings and the homily, we are silent together because we are listening together for the voice on which our very lives depend, the voice that calls us into being, the voice that bids us to come out of our dumb tombs to live and to love again.

On occasion, instead of singing, we may be silent when the gifts of money are gathered for the poor and for the church, and when the gifts of bread and wine are brought to the altar. And when all have been fed, when all have drank from the cup, again we are silent, caught up in the revery of great mystery, standing together wide-eyed and satisfied, breathing quiet gratitude for life breaking out everywhere, enjoying the quiet of this moment before an eternal dawn, when God will be all in all and the final silence will be ruptured with raucous, joyous cries of "Worthy! Worthy! Worthy!"

The liturgy's silences both tax and nourish us. They tire us because they are active moments, concentrated periods of deliberate, attentive, awe-filled stillness. But they nourish us as well. They are vitamins for a life made anemic with noise, tonic for the blathering (the world's and our own) that sometimes sickens us. The moments of communal silence in the liturgy plant seeds of peace in our souls, so that in the turmoil of every day life we can find a still center inside and hear the voice of God.

The Gospel of the Lord!

From the beginning, reading from one of the four gospels has been a high point of our Sunday assembling to give thanks and praise. For good reason, too. Christ comes to us in word as well as in deed, in the scriptures as well as in the sharing of his body and blood. And while we know that God speaks to us in all of holy scripture, at Mass we are most eager to hear the gospel, the good news of the very words and deeds of Jesus. (That is what the Old English word "gospel" means after all, "good news," "God's news.") So when it is time, we jump to our feet. We acclaim the coming of the gospel with that most ancient and holy of words: Alleluia! (Unless it is Lent, our season of sorrow when we fast from our glorious

word just like Israel in exile hung up its harps.) Fast to out feet, singing loud praise, we watch as the deacon (or the priest) takes up the Book of the Gospels. Accompanied by servers with candles, perhaps with fragrant clouds of incense from another server's bowl, the Book of the Gospels makes it way through our assembly from altar to ambo. It sat on the altar from the start of Mass as a sign that Christ is present in the gospel. Now it is taken "up to the heights" to be proclaimed from the ambo, just as Jesus preached the sermon on the mount, or the apostles, drunk with the Holy Spirit, shouted joy from Jerusalem's Pentecost rooftops. As the deacon announces that this is from Matthew or Mark, from Luke or John, we trace the sign of the cross on our foreheads (may we understand this good news!), on our lips (may we always speak and spread this good news!), and over our hearts (may we love and always live this good news!) Then we listen. We stand together and listen. We stand and listen like a servant being given orders, like an honored guest being whose deeds are recounted, like a convicted criminal before the judge's bench, like the beloved being met in haste by the lover. And when it is spoken, when the last word for this day has sunk deep within, the deacon looks to us and says, "The gospel of the Lord!" to which we cry, "Praise to you, Lord Jesus Christ!" What else could we possibly say?

Do We Think That We Change God's Mind?

What do we think we're doing when a we kneel down at the child's bedside and say together, "God bless grandma and grandpa" and "God help Uncle Harry find a job"? Or what is the point of our reader or singer coming forward each Sunday and asking the assembly to pray for this, that and the other thing?

There are lots of valid ways to think about praying for someone or something. One beginning point is the psalms. What strikes me if I recite these ancient Jewish prayers that became the core of the Christian prayer book is this: The person who wrote

But what did they think they were doing? Probably one thing was this: They thought that the church, the body of Christ, was here to shout in God's ear on behalf of all the helpless people, on behalf of the earth itself, on behalf of the living and the dead. Jesus had prayed and now the body of Christ would pray. I don't think ordinary Christians got too wrapped up in questions of what it meant. They just did it. Somebody had to keep reminding God (that's not such a strange way to think: just check out the psalms) that all was not well. Remember us, remember the poor, remember the prisoners.

these prayers was never hesitant to point out to God the urgent concerns of the day. Never. The psalms are full of: Please do this. Do that! Do it now!

And for centuries the churches hardly ever gathered without a time for naming the needs of that day. Mornings, evenings, Sundays. Always the Christians rolled out their list of urgent concerns: peace, health, good weather, strength in the face of hardship, the poor.

This kind of praying was thought of as something a baptized person had to do. It was, in fact, something the unbaptized catechumens were not allowed to do. They couldn't do eucharist, they couldn't give the peace greeting, and they had to be sent out before the baptized people did those intercession prayers. It was that important.

No one ever said: It isn't working, folks, let's quit. We pray and pray and there are still poor people, still sick people, still all kinds of evil. But interceding was what Christians did—like living thankfully, like sharing with those in need. The baptized were trained in this kind of praying.

So are we. In our parish book of prayer, in our book of the names of the dead, with our children at bedside each night, with the sick when we visit them, by ourselves—and here in our liturgy every Sunday week after week. Year after year, can we get louder? Put more of our heart and soul in these prayers?

26

Q&A: My Own Cup?

Why don't we use small individual cups for each communicant? Wouldn't that be more sanitary?

At the last supper, the Lord not only told the disciples to eat of the bread which was his body, but he also said, "Drink from this cup, all of you; for this is my blood of the covenant" (see Matthew 26:27). The practice of all communicants receiving communion from the cup, a custom continued without interruption in most of the Eastern Churches, was reintroduced into the Roman liturgy after the Second Vatican Council and has been encouraged as a visible way of fulfilling one of the Lord's commands to his followers.

But we should remember that sharing communion through receiving the blood of the Lord is more than swallowing a bit a consecrated wine. It is a encounter in faith, rather than a moment of refueling. Thus questions about how the "cup of blessing which we bless" is shared among those assembled for the eucharist must be asked in the context of the biblical and liturgical meaning of this action. We should avoid making religious judgments based on modern American concerns about hygiene or based on the culture of individualism that pervades many aspects of our society and its practices.

There is a long tradition, based on Saint Paul's words to the Corinthians (1 Corinthians 10:16–17), about using one loaf and one cup whenever possible at the eucharist to symbolize the unity of all assembled in the one body of Christ. Anything that unnecessarily disturbs the symbols of unity or values efficiency over authenticity should be avoided.

When many people share communion by drinking from a common cup, they show their commitment to a common enterprise, and, in a sense, respond to the Lord's invitation to James and John: "Can you drink of the cup I am to drink of?" (Matthew 20:22).

We should never be cavalier about health concerns, yet neither should we be paranoid about inflection at every corner. The results of repeated tests by health officials indicate that the possibility of transmitting diseases by drinking from the common cup is almost non-existent when standard precautions are taken (that is, when the lip of the cup is wiped dry and the cup rotated after each communicant).

The eucharist is Christ's gift to his church to nourish us and unite us through our sharing in the one loaf and the one cup. As Saint Augustine wrote, it is a "sign of unity and a bond of charity" which helps build up the one body of Christ. Whenever possible, ritual practices, particularly at communion time, should reinforce, through symbol, the unity we celebrate!

27

Walk the Walk

Our Roman way of doing liturgy may come in as a poor second in rhythmic chanting to African ceremony, or as a poor second in graceful movement to Asian rituals, but there's one category where we ought to win every time: processions.

The church of Rome has processions in its soul. They're written all over the rubrics of the Mass and sacraments. Those early Roman Christians never needed pews or kneelers because they hardly ever came to a stop, except standing around the table.

How strange it is then to see what we've come to in the late twentieth century. Sedentary or standing still. Kneeling. The only processions we do today are fossils of what once was our primary way to do liturgy. Instead of the whole people on the move, we send out a few children leading an ordained priest. And then the rest of us watch. Or we don't. Entrance procession, procession with the gifts, exit procession. Tokens! (Even if we add a gospel procession, it's still not much!)

And what of the one procession that's left to us, the communion procession? It lost its momentum in the centuries when no one came to communion. Now, when the assembly is again ready to approach the table, we can hardly remember what a good procession looks like. There's music, which is what any procession needs. There's order. There's a great circling of our church space, a great chance to be conscious of each other and to know just how wondrous is the body of Christ.

We do pretty well here at St. Nicholas in Evanston, Illinois. Visitors remark that we don't seem like we're in such a terrible hurry when we come forward to communion. There's attention on lots of faces, song in lots of throats. There's such a reverence in the way each processing person comes to the minister and the bread, comes to the minister and the cup. They look at each other and speak without hurrying. The body of Christ. The blood of Christ. Amen! Amen! Nor are people rushing over each other getting back to their places or out the doors. It is a good and holy time. You can almost feel the peace and compassion in this room as the procession ends and we sit and keep some silence together.

This is so in other parishes around the country, too. We are on the way from "lining up" to "processing". That's the way from being one solitary soul among a lot of other solitary souls in the same line — to being an assembly of hungry, thirsty, baptized believers who rejoice to come together to the table of the Lord.

Our task is to make the communion procession a real procession, an image of God's people on their way. What would help that? Think about the good things that singing does, about the ways the procession could be more of a procession and less of a lining up. Think about posture—both in the procession and in the pews.

When we walk in this communion procession, we are learning to walk down the street, through the work place, in the home, in the voting booth, in the picket line, in the hospital and jail corridors. This is all our walking, walking to the Lord. Do it well.

28

Until the Fat Lady Sings

You know the line about opera: "It ain't over till the fat lady sings." The same is true about Sunday Mass. And no, the "fat lady" is not the cantor. She's us — all of us — the church! Sated (miraculously with just a morsel and a sip), stuffed on grace, a bit tired from sincere thanksgiving and sustained praise, the assembly has to finish this liturgy before it's over. Would the cast leave before the final curtain? The orchestra before the finale? The team before the final buzzer or last out? At Mass, we are all the cast, all the orchestra, all the team.

The end of Mass comes quickly: After the silent revery that follows communion, there is a prayer and maybe a hymn. Some announcements follow, then a blessing and dismissal, perhaps a final song. So is it really asking too much of each other to see it through to the very end? Sure, you might be blocking in someone's car in the parking lot. But if we all stay till the end, what difference does it make? Of course the little ones are antsy; we all are at this point. A few minutes more won't hurt. (Nor will cries and squirming now.) And yes, not slipping out early means rubbing elbows with everyone, people jamming up at the doors and a procession of cars crawling out of the parking lot, but isn't this a consequence of the communion that we just shared? Isn't this how we know that we are becoming what we have shared: the body of Christ, risen from the dead, going out into the world to give to others what has been given to us?

It's a simple act of kindness — finishing the liturgy before leaving. And if we slow down just enough to finish our liturgy, maybe we'll slowly learn to finish well other things in life, too. And when we learn to relish and not rush the end of things — the last minutes of a movie, the final words of a conversation, the last hand of cards and the final set of pins to knock down — what we are truly learning is to relish and not rush the end of our days — a final act of gratitude that gives God praise.

29

Sunday Mass Times

2/5/09

Here's another way to think about Sunday Mass times. How many liturgies do other churches and synagogues have on Sunday or Saturday?

Why are we different in this regard? Most of them have a tradition of one service. The synagogue has something on Friday night and something Saturday morning, but they aren't the same thing. The same people come (ideally) to both. Both are for the whole congregation. Likewise in some pentecostal churches, the Sunday morning service is not the Sunday night service; you go to both. But most congregations gather just once each Sunday and the time is set and everybody comes to the one service.

That was certainly the Catholic way for centuries. It changed for lots of reasons:

• Some thought the more Masses, the better.

• Some thought that since we were required to go to Mass on Sunday (a commandment of the church), the least the priests could do was have lots of Masses at convenient times: early morning for the morning people, late morning for the night people (and once that was done, God help the pastor who suggested a change!)

• Not everybody in a parish would fit in the church's building at the same time

But maybe being at Sunday Mass isn't about convenience. Maybe the number of Sunday Masses ought to be determined by only one thing: the size of the room and the number of people who come on Sundays. But why?

Because Catholics aren't customers and this parish is anything but a service station where you can drive in and fill up any time. Sure there are inconveniences about a full church: too hot, too long, too messy, too . . . full! But when church is full, isn't there just something wonderful in that room? All those faces, all those ages, all those voices!

Should it be about individual convenience or about the great gathering of this wonderful church? Should we be challenged to build our individual and family Sundays around liturgy? Not easy, but centuries of Catholics did it.

30

Q&A: Less Can Be More?

Isn't it better to have more Sunday Masses than fewer?

To celebrate Mass according to the vision described in the revised liturgical books requires much more energy than in the recent past. Today's celebration requires a coordination of the ministries of several people, including readers, musicians, eucharistic ministers, cantors and choir members. So many pastors and parish councils are faced with a choice between fewer Masses, which may be celebrated with more vibrancy and more participation, and more Masses, some of which may be sparsely attended and may lack even a minimum amount of music and the assistance of other ministers.

If "convenience" were to be an absolute religious value, one might argue that it would be much more convenient merely to permit Mass "attendance" by watching the liturgy on television and distributing communion via the postal service! But our gathering together is more than physical presence or hearing the right words—it is fundamentally a personal and human celebration of love.

A very ancient tradition held as an ideal the celebration of only one eucharist a day in any one community. This ideal is still prescribed by liturgical law for Holy Thursday and Holy Saturday—only with special permission of the bishop can more than one Mass be celebrated on Holy Thursday. This tradition still is the one governing the scheduling of eucharistic liturgies in many Orthodox parishes.

Sunday liturgies should be evaluated based on the norms found in the current Missal, and those norms presuppose the presence of music, of readers, of communion ministers (if enough clerics are not present). If the number of Masses in a given parish means that several Masses are celebrated with very few people present, scattered throughout a cavernous church and without music or assisting ministers, then re-evaluation needs to take place. In some parishes, God may be better praised by scheduling fewer Masses that are well celebrated.

There will continue to be many challenges and changes facing parishes in the years ahead. Some of these challenges will be prompted by a reduced number of active priests available to preside at the eucharist. But even in communities where there is an adequate number of priests, the mere presence of numerous priests should not imply that many Masses should be celebrated each Sunday as well. The only important thing is that each liturgy celebrated on the Lord's Day is prayer-filled, vibrant, reverant and alive with the presence of the risen Lord whose memory we celebrate.

31

Before You Said Amen

During the eucharistic prayer at Mass today, what were you thinking about? What was on your mind from the moment the presider invited everyone to: "Lift up your hearts!" until you sang the "Amen" before the Our Father?

We Catholics say: This is the most holy time. But what does "holy" mean here, and how do you spend that holy time?

Most of us would admit that we tend to wander off a bit at this time on Sunday. Yes, we sing the "Holy Holy" pretty well, perhaps, with a strong "Hosanna in the highest!" But sometimes we don't focus back in until it's time for the Our Father. Where did we go?

We're pretty good at getting on board for the song that begins the liturgy, and sometimes very good at giving full attention to at least one of the readings and maybe the homily. But if someone were to tap you on the shoulder during the Our Father and say: All right, where were you the last five minutes? How would you answer this question?

This is not to ask: What did the priest just do? (We know that!) The crucial question is: After I said "yes" to the invitation to lift up my heart, after we all said "yes" to that, what happened to those hearts? Did they stay "lifted up"?

Come at it this way. What happens in your life, happens with some regularity, that grabs and holds your whole attention — and grabs and hold you? That's what is asked when we are told to lift up our hearts. We are asked not simply to be quite and attention (that can happen at a good movie or concert). For us as baptized people, we are asked to lift up and give to God our whole selves, engaged with all these other selves, around this altar. What's it like to be totally involved in some deed even for a few minutes? Next time, can you enter into the eucharistic prayer in this way?

The Church Prays with Attention

It begins when we say that we are lifting our hearts to the Lord. It ends when we say Amen, then prepare to pray the Lord's Prayer together. In between these are maybe four or five minutes. What happens during this time is the eucharistic prayer.

What is it that is to take place after we say we'll lift up our hearts to the Lord? Most of us would answer: "The consecration — when the presider says 'This is my body' and 'This is my blood.'" And that is right, but only part of what happens. Why are *we* to lift up *our* hearts and to give God thanks and praise? Why involve all of us?

The name of this time in the Mass says it all. This is the eucharistic prayer. "Eucharist" becomes a name for the consecrated bread and wine only because it first means something else. It is a Greek word that needs several English words to translate it. It is blessing. It is giving thanks. It is praise.

So in the eucharistic prayer, these are the things that the church is to do — and more besides. The priest is within the church to pronounce this prayer, to lead this prayer. The whole church is there to enter into the prayer, to acclaim all the blessing, thanks and praise that the priest speaks.

What we know from the New Testament about our eucharistic prayer is that Jesus would take bread or take wine and give thanks to God. Now we do it in memory of Jesus. What persons have you loved? When you remember them, don't you give thanks?

So the eucharistic prayer is filled with thanks for all God's saving deeds, but especially the passion and death and resurrection of Jesus. In it we name our saints, our pope and our bishop, our dead. All the memories come together when we surround the table and pray that these gifts of bread and wine will become for us the body and the blood of Jesus. If we then call the bread and wine "the eucharist" it is because we have prayed this eucharist to God over them.

What Gets Changed?

A few years ago at a parish in Cleveland, some Catholics were interviewed about going to Mass. One of the questions was: "At Mass, when we pray and sing, when the priest stands at the altar and we pray over the bread and wine, when we come to holy communion, what gets changed?"

One middle-aged man named Sam answered quick as a wink and spoke straight from his heart: "What gets changed? Sam! Sam gets changed."

do, we try to live with others the way the gospels and our saints show us. We try to be one of those to whom the Lord will say: "I was hungry and you fed me, thirsty and you gave me a drink, in prison and you visited me."

Baptism got us into this house, this Catholic house. Sunday eucharist trains us in the life and language and loving deeds of Catholics. It gets us around that table where from the first generation of

Now that man, whether he realized it or not, knew the church's theology deep down in his being. He had experience — not just book learning — of the church's theology of the eucharist.

At our baptism, we put on Christ. We died, we renounced, we turned our backs on whole ways of life. If we were baptized as infants, then our parents meant us to enter on such a Catholic life. At baptism, whether as an infant or an adult, the people already baptized took us into a home. And in that home we do the things that Catholics

Christians we've been gathered to give God thanks over bread and wine. Doing that again and again changed Sam. Little by little, it changes us all. The most sacred mystery of the eucharist is that this bread and wine become for us the body and blood of Christ. The most sacred mystery of the eucharist is that we, slackers and sinners all, become the body and blood of Christ. So what gets changed? Sam gets changed.

A Habit of the Catholic Heart

Are we ready to say grace?" Many religious people pause before they eat and pray. Christians do this also. The English word we have for this prayer is "grace"—the same word we use to speak of the way God's love is given to us freely, given without any earning it on our part.

"Grace" comes easily from a Latin word, *gratia,* a word many know from the close Spanish word, *gracias.* This simple word is trying to get hold of what is best in the human spirit. It is that spontaneous "thanks" that is our response to a kindness, some good word or deed with which another person blesses us.

So at table we say grace, we give thanks. Hunger brings us back to the table—even when there's no table at all—and before we take nourishment, we go hungry a moment longer while we give thanks.

What is done before eating is just one tiny moment of what's the deepest Catholic habit. We want "grace" all the time, morning and night, even in hard times. We are a "thanks saying" people. It comes with the territory. We're shaped in giving thanks by the obligation we have to gather at the church's table every Sunday and make the eucharistic, the thanks-giving, prayer before we feast on the body and blood of the Lord.

We're baptized to be Christ's body giving God thanks all the days of our life, being the voice of creation whether we feel like it or not, whether the times are good or awful (thanks can leave lots of room for lament and even—just pray the psalms—some cursing now and then). This is no easy "Hey, thanks a lot!" It is rather the total thanks of those who have been shaped by Christ's passion and death in God's merciful love for the world.

Are We Ready for This Prayer?

Yes, I will lift up my heart. And I will give God thanks and praise. I'll stay awake. I'll listen to every word. I'll sing every acclamation and Amen. Thus I will put energy into praying the eucharistic prayer at Mass on Sunday. I'll bring to it every bit of life. I'll remember everything, especially the hard stuff (after all, at the center of this prayer is a body to be broken for us, a covenant made in the blood of Christ).

from distractions, from anger—I'll come on Sunday knowing in body and soul how hungry I am to hear God's word and hungry to give God thanks and praise and hungry to feast on the body of Christ given for us, the blood of Christ poured out for us.

And I'll never again think that I can do any of this alone. How could I? It is not I who give God thanks and praise, it is the body of Christ that makes this eucharistic

I will be so attentive that when we've finished the eucharistic prayer with a room-shaking Amen, I'll know just how right and good it is to pray the Our Father together, greet one another with Christ's peace, then enter a procession (not a line up, a *procession*) that is singing its way to the table of the Lord.

And I'll come hungry. By some kind of fasting—from food, from entertainment,

praying. All the baptized people in this room put their lives into this prayer that the ordained priest proclaims. And it goes beyond the room. That's why we remember the church all over the world in our prayers for the bishop and the pope, the living and dead.

Am I ready for this prayer? Are *we?*

The Guilt of Us All

As we observe the passion and death of Jesus, we must remember that no one ethnic or religious group of people is responsible for the death of our Savior. He died voluntarily for the sins of all people "at the hands of evildoers" so that we might be saved from eternal death. The use of the words "the Jews" (or similar expressions) in the gospel accounts of Christ's death does not mean that the Jewish people killed Jesus. In the Gospel of John, for example, it is not even clear who "the Jews" that seek Jesus' death are. Certainly Jesus, his mother Mary, the apostles, and most, if not all of the disciples, are also "the Jews." In fact, everyone in the gospel account except Pilate, his wife, and his soldiers are Jews. (Simon was probably a Jew from Cyrene, perhaps in Jerusalem for the holy day. And scripture tells us that Joseph of Arimathea was "a disciple of Jesus," but it doesn't necessarily mean that he wasn't Jewish — he owned a grave in Jerusalem.) To think that the gospel means that the Jewish people — then and now — are responsible for the death of Jesus (and thus today are to be coerced to convert, blamed or condemned) is wrong. It is sinful to twist the sacred scriptures for any purpose of hate, bigotry or prejudice. It is better to recall the words of the prophet Isaiah that we hear on Good Friday: "He was pierced for *our* offenses, crushed for *our* sins . . . the Lord laid upon him the guilt of us *all*."

37

Matthew's Passion in Context

The charge of Christ-killing has given the sin of anti-Judaism its greatest impetus. The author of the gospel of Matthew put a statement on the lips of the angry mob during the sentencing of Jesus—"His blood be upon us and upon our children" (Matthew 27:25). Tragically, history tore the statement from the context and misused it to justify anti-Jewish action. When Matthew's first hearers recalled the prophecy, "If you kill me, you bring innocent blood on yourselves, on this city and on its citizens" (Jeremiah 26:15), they were in a time and place far from ours. It was years ago and miles away. Truth lies in what the words mean *in context*. Only on their own terms can we understand them.

Like the people he evangelized, Matthew was not "anti-Jewish"; he was angry about the way *some* rabbinic schools interpreted the law and applied it in individual cases: This is casuistry. Legal interpretation was an explosive topic among Jews during almost all of the first century. Matthew's community, originally Jewish itself and gradually including Gentiles, was at home in the mixed culture of the Hellenistic world. Matthew wrote possibly in Antioch, Syria, between the years 80 and 90. He knew the neighborhood.

Matthew's hostility to the scribes and Pharisees—especially in the vehement diatribe against them in chapter 23 and in the passion account—has the tone of a ripe casuistic rivalry of schools within Judaism, rather than the tone of extramural anti-Judaism. He thought if he undercut opposing views he could persuade his hearers better than if he just promoted faithful obedience to the law of Christ's heavenly reign, which was his main interest. Matthew wrote vividly about distorted obedience in order not to risk losing adherents by sounding "soft." It was safe to mock other Jews but not to provoke Romans who held the real power. Matthew sought survival. His fear of Rome far exceeded any opposition to scribes or Pharisees.

Like Paul before him and Ignatius after him, the evangelist walked a fine line. He struggled between conservative, pro-Pharisee followers of Jesus on one side and liberal, pro-Gentile, gnostic followers of Jesus on the other. He had a casuistic problem with the former, an ethical problem with the latter, and he tried to open a middle way.

When Matthew's Jesus says, "Woe to you, scribes and Pharisees, you hypocrites" (23:13), today's hearer must consider the casuistic context of first-century schools of legal interpretation. Likewise, when Matthew's Jesus says, "Come, you blessed of my Father. Inherit the kingdom prepared for you from the foundation of the world. For I was hungry and you gave me food" (25: 34f.), today's hearer must consider the ethical context of Jesus' call to discipleship.

In fairness a hearer must not interpret Matthew's story of the passion and resurrection of Jesus (Matthew 26–28) outside the context of the woes and parables that precede it (23–25). Anti-Judaism as we understand it was not present in that context. Therefore, Matthew's passion story does not validate anti-Judaism. It did so neither for the first century nor for today.

38

Mark's "Israel of the Nations"

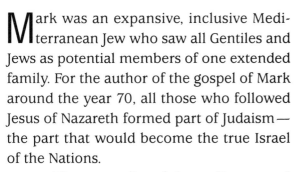

Mark was an expansive, inclusive Mediterranean Jew who saw all Gentiles and Jews as potential members of one extended family. For the author of the gospel of Mark around the year 70, all those who followed Jesus of Nazareth formed part of Judaism — the part that would become the true Israel of the Nations.

The evangelist of the earliest gospel intended his story of Jesus' passion as intramural, intra-Jewish enticement to follow Jesus. He still hoped that members of the establishment, such as the council member from Arimathea (Mark 15:43), would return to the truth. The nameless and named Jewish women who followed Jesus in Galilee and Judea were model forerunners of the true Israel. They included the woman who anointed Jesus at Simon's house in Bethany (14:3–9); the women at the cross (15:40–41), those keeping vigil at the tomb (15:47) and those who found the tomb empty. They ran away saying "nothing to anyone, for they were afraid" (16:8). Truly they were Israel.

For Mark, the inscription of the charge against Jesus, "King of the Jews" (15:26), contained more truth than irony (see 15:2, 18). Compared with the context and tone in the other gospel accounts, the irony here was more hopeful than bitter.

The evangelist interpreted the passion and death of Jesus carefully. Especially with the presence of the Sanhedrin, the account parallels that of the innocent prophet Jeremiah (see Jeremiah 26). Six hundred years earlier Jeremiah threatened destruction for the temple (see Mark 13:1ff.). Priests and others demanded his death. The death of the innocent prophet Jesus was familiar to first-century Jews. Regarding his fellow Jews, Mark's hope was exactly like Jeremiah's long ago: "Perhaps they will listen and turn back, each from his evil way" (Jeremiah 26:3). Jeremiah and Mark reflected a qualified anti-Judaism: disapproval focused on bringing about change.

Not long after the year 70, however, the climate changed. Rome's presence grew much heavier in the small eastern province of the massive empire. Under Roman rule, the evangelists Matthew and Luke developed stronger understandings of discipleship of Jesus as something more churchlike or "Christian." Groups of followers of "the Nazorean" became less like Judaism and more like institutions established alongside it, over it, against it or in competition with it.

The evangelist Mark had a vision of Christianity as a completion of Israel rather than a separation from it. He sought one Israel for the whole world. He certainly would have regretted the schism between rabbinic Judaism and those groups that did not make the "official" cut over the next forty years.

If we allow the gospel of Mark into our hearts, we followers of Christ crucified and risen celebrate the One True Israel. "But we must first preach the gospel to all nations" (Mark 13:10). If the apostle Paul happens by and says, "Peace and mercy be to all who follow this rule and to the Israel of God (Galatians 6:16), our evangelist would reply with full voice, "Amen."

39

Jews and Christians Together in the Gospel of Luke

 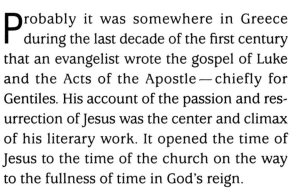

Probably it was somewhere in Greece during the last decade of the first century that an evangelist wrote the gospel of Luke and the Acts of the Apostle — chiefly for Gentiles. His account of the passion and resurrection of Jesus was the center and climax of his literary work. It opened the time of Jesus to the time of the church on the way to the fullness of time in God's reign.

Luke's passion account does not reflect major problems with Judaism, as the other three gospels do. Politically and ethnically, his work is at once simpler and more complex. He knew great varieties of Jewish Christian communities, Gentile Christian communities and mainly mixed Christian communities. For example, in the passion account, "the Jews" occurs three times in a neutral sense (Luke 23:3, 38, 51; 7:3). Even references to the "chief priests" and "scribes" are neutral.

Genuinely positive, however, is Luke's evaluation of the law and the prophets of Israel. At a key transition in the gospel, Jesus affirmed, "Up until John it was the law and the prophets; from that time on the kingdom of God is being preached, and everyone is pressed to enter it" (Luke 16:16). The law and the prophets are not neutral but normative in Luke's view. Justification by faith in Christ, according to the Lucan Paul, is not a replacement of the law, but supplements it (see Acts 13:38–39). In fact the law and the prophets predict truths about God's reign. On the road to Emmaus, for example, the risen Lord, "beginning with Moses and all the prophets, interpreted to them what referred to him in all the scriptures.

"Israel," for Luke, is always the Israel of old, heir of the "promise made to the fathers" (Acts 13:32). The evangelist understood the people of Israel, the Jews, very positively. On one occasion, "three thousand of these Jews welcomed the word and received baptism" (Acts 2:41). Later the number was five thousand (4:4). Finally, "Brother, you see how many thousands of believers there are from among the Jews, and they are all zealous observers of the law" (21:20).

Look at Simeon, Anna, Mary and other faithful people of Israel. Simeon sang out, "My eyes have seen your salvation, which you prepared in the sight of all the people, a light of revelation to the Gentiles, and glory for your people Israel (Luke 3:30ff.; Isaiah 42:6; 46:13; 49:6). John the Baptist proclaimed, "All flesh shall see the salvation of God" (Luke 3:6; Isaiah 40:5).

For Luke, Christians were not the Israel of God, as they were for Paul; nor were they the true Israel of the nations, as for Mark. For Luke, Gentile Christians were part of a larger re-established Israel. Some call it "reconstituted," because the law and the prophets form its "constitution."

Luke's economic vision of Jewish-Christian relations builds on two pillars: the law and the prophets of Israel as well as the paschal mystery of Jesus Christ.

Copyright © 2001 Archdiocese of Chicago: Liturgy Training Publications, 1800 North Hermitage Avenue, Chicago IL 60622-1101; 1-800-933-1800; www.ltp.org. Text by James Wilde. Art by Steve Erspamer, SM. All rights reserved. Used with permission.

40

A Way to Understand John's Bitter Anti-Judaism

Every year on Good Friday we read the passion of our Lord Jesus Christ according to John (John 18:1—19:42). What does the passion account of the Fourth Gospel teach about anti-Judaism? The gospel of John stressed the universal law of love and did not exclude Jews from this love. John encouraged prospective members of his community to make the painful transition away from Jewish institutions, including the temple, synagogue, priesthood and feasts. He asked them to replace Jewish practices with faith in Christ and Christian practices. The "beloved disciple," who likely started the Johannine community, served as the best example of the transition.

In John's passion account (18:1—19:42), there is a small sample of Jewish institutions that received the evangelist's sharp, negative judgment. "Judas the betrayer" arrived with a hostile "band of soldiers and guards from the chief priests and Pharisees," who represented official Jewish institutions. "Jewish guards seized Jesus" (18:12). This is not how other evangelists reported it. Could it be that John's hearers learn more about the last part of the first century here than they do about the actual time of Jesus in the first part of the century? "Caiaphas . . . counseled the Jews that it was better that one man die rather than the people" (18:14). "The Jews" clearly did not receive Jesus, the Messiah, the Son of God. The beloved disciple and the Johannine community did receive him. "The chief priests answered, 'We have no king but Caesar'" (19:15). The evangelist heard this statement as the ultimate blasphemy.

A widely held theory may help to understand these indictments. Members of John's community were Jewish followers of the Nazorean Jesus. Members of the synagogue community expelled them for their faith in him as the Messiah, Son of God. How intense was their subsequent hostility toward that Jewish establishment, from which officials alienated them by force! It matched their bitter disappointment that not only the Jews but the whole world rejected the Word-made-flesh (see 1:10–11). However, their intense anger did not match their strong commitment to Jesus.

The anti-Judaism of John's gospel is not the same as historic and modern anti-Jewish prejudice. Nor can it be used to justify the sin of anti-Judaism. Rather, this hostility reflects less a prejudice and more a "postjudice." It resulted from rejection and expulsion from the parent Jewish community for a strongly held belief. John felt raw human outrage that the cherished Son of God did not find a home where he himself had been at home. His gospel did not model or encourage anti-Judaism for future times. Instead, it encouraged conversion to the love of Jesus. The evangelist took pride in the great examples there were to follow! These included the experiences of the Beloved Disciple, Nicodemus, the Samaritan woman, the man born blind, Joseph of Arimathea, Mary of Magdala, Thomas the twin and Mary the mother of Jesus.

41

Which Three Days Are *The* Three Days?

There's a lot of talk in church now about "the Three Days," or in Latin, the "Triduum." These are our most holy of days. They make up our most important single celebration of the year: Easter. But exactly *which* three days make up the Triduum?

At first this sounds like a stupid question such as, "What color was Napoleon's white horse?" or "Who's buried in Grant's tomb?" Actually, it's a trick question. Most would say that the Three Days are Holy Thursday, Good Friday and Holy Saturday. And that's wrong! (How could Easter Sunday *not* be one of the Three Days?!)

The three days of the Triduum are counted using the Jewish way of keeping time: from sunset to sunset. So the first day of the Triduum is from sunset on Holy Thursday until sunset on Good Friday. The second day is from sunset on Good Friday until sunset on Holy Saturday. The third day is from sunset Holy Saturday (the great Easter Vigil) to sunset Easter Sunday (Paschal Vespers).

Does this make any difference—or is it only good Catholic trivia? Here's the difference that it makes. We tend to think of the Three Days as commemorating separate, distinct events: On Holy Thursday we remember the Last Supper, on Good Friday we recall the passion and on Holy Saturday the resurrection. But in our liturgy, the church thinks about the Last Supper not as the last thing that happened on Holy Thursday, but as the *first* thing to happen on Good Friday. What new insights into the eucharist do you have when you think of it

as the first act of Christ's passion? What new understanding of Sabbath—the day of rest—do you have when you reflect on the fact that Jesus slept in death from sunset Friday and all through the Jewish Sabbath, Saturday? And how might we spend our Saturday nights if we understood them to truly be the beginning of Sunday—not just during the Triduum, but year round? What does it mean when the deacon or cantor sings at the Vigil that because of the resurrection, this night is brighter than any day?

These Three Days are a single moment. We walk (or crawl) into this moment on Thursday night and walk (or dance) out on Easter day. In between, there's a flood of stories and songs, rites and rest, fasting and feasting. The Three Days are time out of time, the center of our year and of our life.

42

Smudged with Ashes, Smeared with Oil

On a somber Wednesday we will gather to smudge every forehead with ashes, admonishing each other to remember that dust returns to dust and that the only way through death to life is Christ. The ashes are made by burning palms — given to us on Passion Sunday a year ago with the invitation to "go forth in peace, praising Jesus our Messiah, as did the crowds that welcomed him into Jerusalem." Our baptismal life is a lifelong pilgrimage with Christ toward Jerusalem. Yet like our best intentiuons, last year's palm branches now have become dried and brittle — fodder for the fire. So our pilgrimage leads us to Lent. And a hostile climate of sin and suffering necessitates drastic measures: We are marked with ashes as a sign of our willingness to pray, fast and give alms.

But this gritty smudge that we accept on our foreheads is not a death sentence. It is not the mark of Cain. A reminder of our fragile mortality, it is nonetheless shaped in the great sign of salvation: The ashes form a cross, a thumb-printed cross that marks the same heads that were smeared with chrism at baptism. Anointed with that royal oil, we are committed to conversion, to continually setting out for the new Jerusalem, to leaving behind forever our captivity in Egypt.

This gritty ashen sign reminds us that on the way there is soil and toil, sweat and hard work before we come to the oasis in this desert — the Easter bath of baptism. At the font, on a damp and chilly night, water will wash away soil and oil will soothe away toil to make new Christians royal: heirs of the reign of God. The dusty smudges will be gone, and in the light of the paschal candle the oily heads of the newly baptized will shine like the moon and the stars, reminding us of our destiny. What begins in ashes ends in water and in fire.

43

Pilgrims, Palms, Processions

Next Sunday is Palm Sunday, and we will meet outside of our normal place of worship to hear about how Jesus entered Jerusalem in triumph before his passion, death and resurrection. Then we will bless palm branches—branches carried by us as pilgrims. And like the children of Jerusalem we will walk and sing in procession. The gospel that we have been listening to all year long now has been leading us to this journey to Jerusalem, this procession to the supper table, the cross and the tomb.

When we accept the palm branches next week, we promise to live as pilgrims, to move through this life with and to Jesus. Like the Israelites in the desert, we are only passing through. Like Christ himself, we go about carrying good news, even when we walk the way of tears. Come prepared next week to walk and sing together as fellow travelers. We will walk behind our cross to our holy table—Jerusalem, in our own neighborhood. And this procession will be practice for an even more awesome journey that we will make in two weeks—the Easter Vigil's procession to the font of baptism— that place where we die to sin and rise in love to life everlasting.

44

Holy Days in History

Sunday is our original—and at first our only—holy day. As time went on, some churches began keeping other days holy, too: days to remember an event in the life of Christ or Mary, or the anniversary of the death of saint.

In medieval Europe, these "feast days" were important. There was no such thing as a "weekend." Every day—except Sunday—was a long and hard work day. A feast day meant that you only had to do the most necessary work. Then you could go to town for Mass, for socializing, playing, resting. It didn't take long for feast days to multiply. Every so often the church would have to cut back the number, or else folks would go four or five days without working! Feast days were possible because most everyone in a locale was Catholic.

When Spanish Catholics came to North America, they tended to create Catholic towns. Many Native Americans, too, live in Catholic communities. To this day the pueblos of New Mexico still keep feast days with dancing and special foods. French Catholics, especially in Canada, kept alive some of their holy days. But Catholics from other countries lived in mixed communities with people of different religions. They could not close their stores because it was Ascension Thursday, or not help neighbors raise a barn on All Saints. Not until the great Catholic neighborhoods formed in the bigger cities could Catholics close up shop, go to morning Mass, and then spend the day feasting and relaxing—even on a week day!

Bishops began to designate certain holy days as "holy days of obligation." Usually these were feast days that were already popular in a given community. The number of holy days that Catholics observed in the United States varied until 1885. Then, six days were set: January 1, Ascension Thursday (a different date each year), August 15, November 1, December 8 and December 25. Prior to this, how many and which holy days you kept depended on whether you lived in English, Spanish or French America. For example, English-speaking Catholics had 11 holy days of obligation from 1777 until 1885.

As our neighborhoods and parishes change, so do our rules about keeping holy days. In 1969, the bishops decided to transfer our solemn celebration of the Lord's Epiphany from January 6 to the Sunday that falls nearest before that date. Epiphany is an important holy day, and yet the whole Catholic community can not count on having January 6 free. Recently, the bishops have voted to move our solemn celebration of the Lord's ascension from a Thursday to a Sunday: the Seventh Sunday of Easter. This change should allow all of us to keep this holy feast day with Mass, recreation and feasting, as we give thanks and praise for all that God does for us in Christ Jesus, our risen Lord.

45

Day or Date?

One of the first debates in the early church was this: Should we celebrate Easter each year on the date that Christ rose from the dead (the fourteenth day of the Jewish month named Nisan, according to the gospel of John), or should we celebrate it each year on the day of the week that he rose from the dead—Sunday? Some of the churches in Asia said "date." After all, Jesus' rising from the dead changed history, and we ought to keep this date holy. (And this is what the churches later decided to do with Christmas, which we celebrate every year on December 25, no matter what day of the week it is.) The church in Rome said "day": Sunday—the Lord's Day—is the best time to keep the solemn feast of the resurrection. Sunday was our first—and for a century or so, only—holy day. How could Easter not be on a Sunday? Rome won the debate. To this day, all churches celebrate Easter on a Sunday, and never on a weekday.

Recently, the bishops of the United States had a similar discussion: Should we continue to keep the solemn feast of the Lord's Ascension on a Thursday—the fortieth day after Easter, according to the Acts of the Apostles—or should we move it to a Sunday, the Lord's Day? (In the gospels of Mark and Luke, Jesus ascends into heaven on a Sunday.) A few years back, the bishops in the western states and in Canada wanted to try celebrating Ascension on Sunday instead of Thursday. Rome approved their plan as an experiment to see if more people would be able to participate in Mass if Ascension Day was a Sunday. It worked. So the bishops of the US discussed whether the whole country should switch the Ascension from a Thursday to a Sunday. They agreed to make the choice region by region, and not for the whole United States. Rome approved.

So this year, Ascension Day takes the place of the Seventh Sunday of Easter. The psalm for this solemn feast bids us to sing: "God mounts his throne to shouts of joy, a blare of trumpets for the Lord! All you peoples, clap your hands. Sing praise!" Sunday is the Lord's Day and the Ascension into heaven is the Risen Lord's glory. Let us all keep holy this great feast of our God.

46

Halloween and All Saints

Halloween is the eve of Hallowmass, better known to modern Christians as All Saints' Day. Hallowmass celebrates God's harvesting into heaven the faithful of every age, culture and walk of life. It is a day of glorious rejoicing.

Saints are people who, by their joyful service, have extended the love of God to others. The Roman martyrology—the list of the saints officially recognized as such by the church—contains over ten thousand names. And those are only the saints whose names we remember! All Saints' Day also remembers those holy people whom no one but God any longer knows. The reading for the day from the Book of Revelation describes "a great multitude that no one could count."

The abundance of the harvest of souls is perfectly suited to observance in the northern hemisphere in late autumn. That's why in North America All Saints' Day and Halloween are brightened with corn shocks, pumpkins, apples, nuts and other signs of nature's bounty.

The American tradition of Halloween ghost-and-goblin madness comes from Celtic lands, where the spirits of the dead were thought to roam the earth for one night before winter began. To ward off their fear of the supernatural, people sat around huge bonfires, telling stories and sharing the fruits of the harvest. Children were sent round to beg for fuel for the fire. Although the practice of "trick-or-treating" has its roots in pre-Christian Celtic tradition, it would be a mistake to write off the practice as devil worship. In Christ, all things have been made new. And so we dress as ghosts and goblins to laugh at the devil, who has lost ultimate power over God's beloved children.

In Mexico, especially in the southern state of Oaxaca, families go and tend the graves of their loved ones at this time of year. In the middle of Halloween night, they have a fiesta with masks, food, sweets (like miniature skulls made of candy) and bunches upon bunches of marigolds—all by the light of candles in the cemetery! Those who have gone before us, marked with the sign of faith, are still members of the family!

47

When Was Jesus Born?

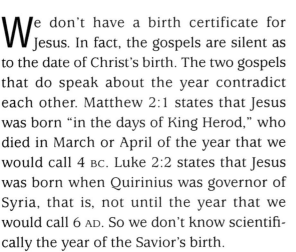

We don't have a birth certificate for Jesus. In fact, the gospels are silent as to the date of Christ's birth. The two gospels that do speak about the year contradict each other. Matthew 2:1 states that Jesus was born "in the days of King Herod," who died in March or April of the year that we would call 4 BC. Luke 2:2 states that Jesus was born when Quirinius was governor of Syria, that is, not until the year that we would call 6 AD. So we don't know scientifically the year of the Savior's birth.

What about the date — December 25? It's possible that this is Jesus' birthday. We know that some churches kept December 25 as the solemn feast of the nativity very early on. Maybe they knew something that we don't. Some think that there are other reasons why December 25 has been kept as Jesus' birthday at least since the year 336.

Some scholars think that Christians began celebrating the birth of Christ on December 25 because it was the pagan feast of the Unconquered Sun, proclaimed by the Roman emperor in the year 274. According to the calendar at the time, December 25 would have been the winter solstice, the shortest day of the year, when hours of sunlight stop "shrinking." (December 21 is the solstice on modern calendars.) Since Christians knew that *Jesus* was truly the Unconquered Sun of Justice, what better day to feast his birth in the flesh?

Another group of scholars think that the early Christians thought: "The gospels say nothing of Christ's birthday, but John the Baptist, as usual, points to the truth. He says 'Christ must increase, but I must decrease.' (John 3:30) Now we can figure out Jesus' birthday!" John the Baptist was hinting that his birthday was the summer solstice — the longest and brightest day of the year — June 25 on the old calendar. (In fact, we still celebrate the birth of the Baptist on June 24!) After all, John is the brightest and strongest of the prophets to foretell Christ's coming. So this means that John would have been conceived on September 25. Being a holy saint, he would have been in Elizabeth's womb for exactly nine months. Luke 1:26 tells us that John was conceived six months prior to Jesus. So Jesus was conceived on March 25. Being the Son of God, Christ is the perfect human being, so of course he was in Mary's womb exactly nine months, and thus born on December 25.

Sadly, there are still those today who won't believe that Jesus even existed until they see some kind of birth certificate. But we who are baptized are open to other ways of knowing truths bigger than official documents and laboratory-evidence can tell. We learn in our liturgy to sense divine action in human history. We know that we can trust our church calendar, waiting in Advent, rejoicing at Christmas, joyfully celebrating God in the flesh — our flesh — born into our world, redeeming even our calendars, giving us holidays to cherish. Today is born our Savior, Christ the Lord!

48

To Eat or Not to Eat

The original sin is eating that which is forbidden. But the first creatures disobedience is reversed by the obedience of Jesus who refrains from all food and drink for forty days in the desert. For the followers of Jesus no blessings of creation are forbidden. Taking up the Lenten fast, therefore, demands an examination of our assumptions about his discipline of restraint.

Our assumptions are revealed in our language. We say about rich chocolate desserts that they are "sinful." Do we assume that the eating of anything so luscious and delightful is lacking in virtue? Do we harbor some suspicion that God does not delight in our taking delight?

God truly rejoices in our happiness. One paradox of fasting is that in refraining from that which we enjoy day after day we come to cherish and value it even more. This is not unlike the deeper appreciation we have for friends and loved ones who move away or die. In a very real sense the festal excess of Easter depends upon the joyful restraint of Lenten fasting.

One of the prefaces of the eucharistic prayer call Lent "this joyful season." Christian fasting allows the pangs of separation from snacks and even meals to trigger a sense of thanksgiving to God who has given us such delights.

How can fasting be a joyful practice instead of a burdensome obligation?

49

Spiritual Carrots

Carrots supposedly help your eyesight. Fasting helps your vision! Vision is acquired and shaped. We learn to see and learning to recognize the real from the unreal demands discipline. Art experts spend a lifetime learning to distinguish authentic paintings from fakes and reproductions.

The preface to the eucharistic prayer today proclaims that Jesus had to teach his disciples that "the promised Christ first had to suffer and so come to the glory of his resurrection." While preparing them for his death, he revealed himself in glory. Fasting is certainly a way of dying to self. Can it also reveal Christ's glory within us?

The transfigured body of Christ was a foretaste of his risen glory. Our engagement in fasting is a participation in the freedom promised us at baptism. God's gifts are good but too often these goods are made by us into little gods who rule and dominate our lives. We are often ruled by the desires fueled within us by images of food and drink served up by TV, radio and magazines. Fasting is an exercise in freedom. It is a death to what we want in order to discover our deepest and truest needs. At the center we discover the glory of Christ who strengthens us in all our dyings.

What one thing is fasting helping you to see more clearly?

50

Spiritual Direction

One of the more positive developments of our times is the rebirth of the tradition of spiritual direction. Wise and holy men and women agree to become "soul friends" to other Christians discerning God's will in their lives. One of the most important questions in this spiritual walk is this: "What is the deepest desire of your heart?" The question is not so easily answered. What first pops to mind is invariably found to be a secondary or tertiary desire rooted in a deeper and more fundamental one.

The Samaritan woman at the well was having an intense experience of spiritual direction. Jesus was helping her to become aware of the deepest desires of her hearts. Serial husbands were simply a symptom of something more basic.

Fasting connected to prayer is a traditional discipline of spiritual direction. Willingness to reflect on my insatiable desire for a pizza before bedtime can become a moment of deeper revelation. Perhaps the insight will be as seemingly embarrassing as coming to know that food is a temporary relief from loneliness. Living without that easy relief may help me to see my disconnectedness from friends, family, parish and the master who waits for me at the well.

From what does your use of food and drink give you temporary relief? What might you do about these deeper desires?

51

Experiencing Hunger

In fasting we voluntarily accept a state of hunger which millions of our brothers and sisters are forced to accept every day of their often all too brief lives. Fasting is thus a privileged entry into the experience of a vast portion of the human family with whom we seldom associate. In sharing their experience we come to an understanding of their plight unavailable to those who simply think about the sufferings of the poor. We might even say that this experiential knowledge makes all other knowledge seem like blindness about their world.

The season of Lent is a time of coming to fresh clarity about the responsibilities which we accept at baptism. The man born blind and given vision by Jesus almost immediately found himself in trouble as a result of his new sight and its source. Those who willingly accept the hungers of the poor will undoubtedly be led to address the needs of their brothers and sisters. Thus the connection between fasting and alms.

Fasting, however, is not just a way to raise social consciousness. It is a trigger which brings us to new thankfulness for the gifts God has given us and which Christ asks us to share that we might embody our communion with all God's children.

What does it feel like to be truly hungry and thirsty?

52

Fasting Together

Christians who have done any study of Paul know that "flesh" for Paul is not the same as "body." "Flesh" is what keeps us centered upon ourselves. When we are caught in old habits of self-centeredness we often know how helpless we are, how dead to the Spirit moving within us. Especially when such self-centeredness becomes or even borders on addiction we feel trapped, imprisoned, entombed. In that state of need we cry out for someone to set us free.

We are past the halfway mark of that time of year when we declare in each Sunday's rite of scrutiny that God has given us one another as the Spirit-empowered instruments of liberation for one another. No one does this work of freedom alone. Fasting is a privileged kind of communion. It is a shar-ing of need, a celebration of absence. This aspect of Catholic spirituality is as necessary to our common life of faith as rests are in music, as voids in sculpture, as silence in prayer.

Prayer is always joined to fasting. Fasting triggers in this season a remembrance to pray for those being brought to the font, to full communion or to reconciliation. Only after we have shared the absence can we come with full hearts to the paschal banquet.

What can I do to fast in communion with others?

53

Stand Watch

In the ancient world the soldier who kept the night watch was said to be on station. He neither slept nor ate but kept his whole attention on looking out for friend or foe who might approach the gates of the city or camp. The church took over that vocabulary. Stational liturgy, when the bishop presides at the eucharist of the local church, is the fullest form of communal prayer for us. Its derivative form will take place in every parish where the pastor presides at the sacraments of initiation at the Easter Vigil. For centuries the candidates, the ministers and the rest of the local church fasted together and saw their fasting as a necessary element of the celebration.

The original Lenten fast was that of Holy Saturday and through the night which opened onto Easter morning. To that was added the fast of Good Friday. The fast of this Holy Week is not so much an acceptance of physical pain in order to know the suffering of Jesus. It is much more an entrance into a state of heightened awareness triggered by our hunger. The pain in the belly calls us to be on the lookout for the glorious coming of Christ into the lives of those whom God has called to join our number. For those who have observed the Lenten fast as well as for those who have done little or no fasting the closing days of this week call us all to stand and watch.

How faithful have I been to fasting this Lent? How can I redouble my efforts in these last days?

54

Water

A glorious and lovely custom, the origins of the Easter bath date back a little more than thousand years, from the time that large numbers of eastern Europeans first accepted Christianity and were baptized into the faith.

The custom takes many forms. It can be as sensuous as taking a warm, perfumed bath by candle light. And it can be as silly as tossing water balloons on the unsuspecting.

Water is precious to Christians. It reminds us of the rivers of paradise, the great flood and the Red Sea. In baptism we enter those waters to be created anew. In baptism we are led safely to freedom. Baptismal waters are like a tomb. In them we die, are buried and are raised with Christ. The waters are like a womb. In them we are reborn.

Throughout Eastertime, the 50 days from Easter until Pentecost, on the feast of the Baptism of the Lord each January and on the actual anniversary of your own celebration of the first sacrament, remember and renew your baptism. Ask parents and godparents what they can recollect about it. What mementoes can you find—your robe, candle or certificate?

Set a bowl brimming with water on the kitchen table. Morning and night, take some water on your fingertips and make the sign of the cross as a pledge of resurrection.

55

Bread

In the old days, before yeast was readily available at markets, many households kept some alive in a crock stored somewhere warm in the kitchen. The yeast was tended by adding flour and water as needed. A bit of it leavened each batch of bread dough. Eventually bacteria would get into leaven, which made it stink to high heaven. What's worse, contaminated leaven failed to make bread rise. So it got thrown out and some was borrowed from a neighbor to start fresh. At Passover, the Jewish people make a communal ritual of this new beginning by tossing out the old leaven and by eating unleavened bread until new yeast develops.

For Christians, the action of fresh yeast is an emblem of resurrection and a sign of the life-giving Spirit. Saint Paul told the Corinthians to throw out the old yeast so that the new—the gospel—could raise them up.

With your companions (a word that means "those we break bread with"), celebrate the season with Easter breads, perhaps with a *babka, brioche, lambropsomo* (Greek "shining bread"), hot cross buns or *colomba di Pasqua* (Italian "Easter dove"). These can be savory symbols of the bread of life, the risen Christ, who is made known to us in the breaking of the bread.

56

Wine

Through fermentation, yeasts convert the sugar in grapes into carbon dioxide and other byproducts, including alcohol. There is obvious energy in this transformation. Fermenting grapes hiss and fizz with potentially explosive force. In Christian tradition, wine has become symbolic for the power of the Holy Spirit.

God's Spirit is the lifeblood of the body of Christ. Jesus commands us to drink deeply. On Pentecost the disciples drank so much of the Spirit that bystanders thought they were drunk. The pentecostal signs of the Spirit, such as fire and wind, share qualities in common. Like wine, they can be agents of destruction or forces for creativity and delight.

During Eastertime it seems as if the earth itself is filled with these signs. Orchards and vineyards blossom. Sunshine pours down and gentle breezes blow. And, on occasion, there are windy thunderstorms and even worse. Keep people in your prayers whose lives are disrupted when the weather turns wild.

Throughout Eastertime, celebrate the Spirit with kites and windsocks, with maywine and sweet liqueurs, with fiery barbecues and flickering candles. Make of this season a time to turn away from destruction and to renew your powers of creativity and delight. In the eucharistic feast, drink deeply of the Spirit.

57

Wood

On Good Friday two crisscrossed planks of lumber were carried into church. A voice sang out, "This is the wood of the cross, on which hung the Savior of the world." And all of us gathered there stepped forward to give glory to God by venerating this holy wood.

For us Christians, wood calls many things to mind: A cypress ark saved creation from the flood. Moses held high his walking stick to divide the sea. When God asked Abraham to sacrifice his son Isaac, the boy carried the wood for his own funeral pyre. But God chose life, not death, for Abraham's beloved son.

There is a legend that the cross of Christ was hewn from Eden's long-dead tree of life. The blood of Christ brought this wood to life so that it flowered afresh.

In your home, honor the life-giving cross. Hang it in the place you pray. If you have no cross, a couple of branches would make a fine one. During this Easter season keep some spring flowers alongside it.

Friday is Arbor Day in many places. Celebrate the resurrection by planting a tree. Give God glory that two ordinary pieces of wood have become a promise of paradise.

Wax

Eastertime is the 50-day-long season from Easter Sunday until Pentecost, May 22 this year. Throughout this time the paschal candle shines in church. This candle is an image of the risen body of Christ. It was kindled and consecrated with great ceremony on Easter Eve.

When people are baptized into the church, they are given candles lit from the paschal candle. They are told to keep their lamps burning brightly throughout their lives. At funerals the paschal candle shines on the dead, like a pillar of fire to guide them to the promised land.

A burning candle is a sign of self-sacrifice. It consumes itself in a blaze of glory. Traditionally, the church's candles are made from beeswax. A beehive is a symbol of the church, where everyone is called to work together for the common good.

Many households light a fine, fat candle every mealtime, and indeed, every time they gather to pray. It is a holy habit.

When you light a candle in prayer you might say, "Jesus Christ is the light of the world, a light no darkness can extinguish." Or say the words proclaimed at the Easter Vigil, "Light of Christ! Thanks be to God!"

59

Incense

"Let my prayer rise before you like incense." Each evening the church sings these words from Psalm 141. That's one reason we Christians praise God with incense: It is a sign of prayer.

The smoke of melting incense is also a sign of sacrifice, of purification, of homage, of mystery. It calls to mind the bright cloud of God's presence that filled the holy of holies within the Temple in Jerusalem. At the transfiguration and ascension of Jesus, his body was surrounded by a cloud. Perhaps that is why some people imagine heaven to be a place of shining clouds where the angels glorify God with incense.

When Ascension is kept on a Thursday, it is the fortieth day of the Easter season. It is like a Lord's Day in the middle of the week. When Ascension is kept on a Sunday, it replaces the Seventh Sunday of Easter. Therefore, as with every Lord's Day, we are given a holy time for worship, recreation, renewal and, today at least, for a bit of restful cloud gazing.

After a festive supper on Ascension, burn some incense (available at religious goods stores). You can do this most simply by heating the incense in an old pan. Or have a barbecue Thursday night and toss some incense on the burning coals. Ascend with Christ into the sweet-smelling clouds of heaven.

60

Oil

Besides being used in cooking, olive oil is an old-fashioned ointment for burns and bruises. In fact, some drug stores still sell it as a medicine.

The Good Samaritan poured oil and wine on the wounds of the man who was attacked by robbers. The Letter of James tells the church to anoint the sick with oil. These scriptures are a foundation for the church's sacrament of the sick. Through this holy anointing, people who are sick unite their suffering with Christ.

Before competition, athletes may limber their muscles with an oily rubdown to make their bodies shine. That ancient practice is the origin of the church's oil of catechumens (who are people preparing for baptism). Catechumens take part in a kind of competition. They grapple with faith. They struggle against evil.

In preparation for Pentecost, treat yourself to a bottle of fine olive oil. Savor its fragrance and unique flavor.

The church's use of olive oil brings to mind Noah's darling dove, which bore in its beak an olive branch as a sign of peace, of earth touching heaven. We Christians are anointed with oil so that our bodies, with all our sufferings and struggles, become bearers of the olive branch, become shining signs of peace.

61

Chrism

"Christening" is a wonderful, old word for the sacraments of baptism, confirmation and eucharist. These are the three sacraments that initiate us into the church. To be christened is to be made a *Christianos,* a "new Christ."

When Jesus was baptized in the Jordan River, God anointed him with the Holy Spirit. The word "christ" means "anointed." The church anoints the baptized with chrism, which is oil mixed with perfume, as a sacramental sign of the outpouring of the Spirit.

Saint Paul tells us that "we are the aroma of Christ" (2 Corinthians 2:15). It is no wonder then that the church uses the sense of smell in the worship of God. Fragrance can be invisible evidence.

In spring we often are surrounded with christening aromas wafting through our windows, of sweet lilacs and crab apples, of iris and peonies, of all the grace-filled scents and sights of the awakening land. Perhaps each morning in the shower, with simple water and scented soap, you can renew your christening.

In whatever you do, uncover evidence of Easter. Search for the signs of the Spirit, who has been sent to renew the face of the earth.

Blessed Brother André

He didn't die a martyr's death. He was too sickly, weak and awkward to do any work except as a porter. Yet, at his death in 1937, over a million pilgrims filed past his coffin. And thousands upon thousands come to Montreal each year to ask the intercession of Saint Joseph and Brother André at the great oratory built by the humble little porter of Notre-Dame-du-Sacré-Coeur.

Born near Montreal in 1845, Alfred Bessette was orphaned by age twelve. Although his frail condition made it impossible to find gainful employment, his pastor, seeing the intensity of his spiritual life, introduced him to the Congregation of the Holy Cross.

In 1870, bearing a letter of recommendation from his pastor stating, "I am sending you a saint," Alfred asked to be accepted into the novitiate. In the novitiate he finally learned to read. Alfred eventually memorized long passages of scripture, including all four gospel accounts of the passion of Christ. However, his health remained so poor that he was only allowed to make final vows in 1872 through the intervention of the bishop of Montreal; he took the name André, after his pastor. For most of his life, he served as porter of the College of Notre-Dame-du-Sacré-Coeur in Cote-des Nieges, near Montreal. He is quoted as saying: "At the end of my novitiate, my superiors showed me the door, and I stayed there for forty years."

It soon became evident that Brother André had been given extraordinary gifts of healing and counselling. Countless are the stories of healings told by students and visitors alike. Numbers grew so large, so quickly that opposition to his ministry arose: partly out of jealousy and scepticism and partly due to fears of contagion among the masses of sick seeking his help.

Brother André's dream was to build a chapel dedicated to Saint Joseph as a spiritual center for those who came for help. He eventually obtained permission to raise the money to build on land on Mount Royal that the Congregation had purchased in 1896. First, in 1904, came a small shelter, 15 by 18 feet. But by 1966 it had grown into a basilica.

On January 6, 1937, the sickly Brother André died at the advanced age of 91. Brother André's simplicity gives hope to those who feel that a lowly state in life — whether physical, financial or educational — might limit their personal gift to the world. In today's economy-driven culture, his life stands as a counter-sign to those who would define power in terms of might and economic prowess. We celebrate his memory each year on January 6.

Saint Marguerite Bourgeoys

Born in France in 1620, Marguerite Bourgeoys is claimed by Canadians by virtue of her nearly forty-seven-year ministry in and around early Montreal. The Congregation of Notre Dame, which she founded, was the first Canadian religious community and today continues the spread of the message of God's love across Canada and around the world.

Marguerite took a private vow of chastity at the age of 23, but eventually carved out a new style of "religious life." She and her companions would not live in a cloister; rather, they adopted the dress of the poor and actively engaged society.

In 1642 Governor de Maisonneuve invited her to teach among his people in New France. And so it began. With nothing but a small bundle under her arm, Marguerite travelled to the new land. Immediately she began to serve whatever needs she discerned in the tiny village. She began the first school there in a stone stable, offering education to poor and working class children and opened a vocational school for young girls sent from France to become brides for the settlers, offering them both practical and spiritual guidance.

To meet the varied needs of the community, Marguerite managed to complete several building projects by bartering with tradesmen; she and her companions were not above doing backbreaking menial labor alongside them in order to speed the job along. That most of these buildings were begun without the finances in sight for completing them attests to her abiding trust in God. Her "magnum opus" in this endeavour was the chapel, Notre Dame de Bon Secours, built as place of pilgrimage in honor of Mary.

Marguerite demonstrated a total commitment to work for that for which she prayed, no matter how distasteful or burdensome the work. She would be quite at home today in Canada's inner cities. Her hands-on approach to addressing social ills is carried on in the lives of teachers and social

activists, as well as in the vibrant community she founded. We celebrate her memory on January 12.

Blessed Kateri Tekakwitha

Tekakwitha was born in 1656 in Ossernenon, a Mohawk village in upper New York, where Isaac Jogues met his death. Her mother was a devout Catholic of the Algonquin nation but had been taken captive in a war with the Mohawks. Tekakwitha's father was a Mohawk chief. When a smallpox epidemic wiped out most of her people, including both her parents as well as her brother, Tekakwitha survived with very bad eyesight and a scarred body.

Though her mother was Catholic, Tekakwitha had never been baptized. Now, orphaned at age 4, she was adopted by her father's family, who hated the Jesuit missionaries. But after a peace treaty allowed the Jesuits to preach in the Mohawk villages, Tekakwitha met with them in secret and at the age of 20 was baptized and given the name Kateri, for Catherine.

Kateri cherished time spent in the woods walking and kneeling for hours in prayer. But she was harshly punished for refusing to work on Sundays and for refusing to marry. Punitive beatings, continual criticism, and mockery were constant. In 1677, seeing her perseverance and fortitude, one of the Jesuits decided to send her away to Kahnawake in Quebec, where there was a large community of Christian aboriginal people. There she was able to express and deepen her faith freely. Kateri lived a life dedicated to care for the sick and aged, prayer, and severe penitential practices.

When Kateri visited Montreal she witnessed Marguerite Bourgeoys and her companions working and living in a convent. On her return, Kateri, along with a widowed companion, tried to convince the priest to open a convent in the village. Finally, in 1679 she was allowed to begin a small convent at the mission.

However, in the spring of 1680, Kateri's health deteriorated rapidly. Her pain soon became so great that she was not able to move. When she died at the age of 24, her last words were "Jesus and Mary." Those at her side said that as they watched all the scars on her body disappeared and her disfigured face and skin shined.

Kateri was the first of the aboriginal people of North America to be beatified. She is invoked as patroness of the environment and ecology. In Canada, she is remembered each year on April 17, and in the United States on July 14.

65

Saint Marguerite D'Youville

Born in 1701 at Varennes, Quebec, Marie Marguerite Dufrost de Lajemmarais was well educated and endowed with an independent spirit. But, through the years of persecution and tribulation that were to come, Marguerite's trust in the love of God never flagged, nor did her determination to serve.

In 1722 she entered into an unfortunate marriage to Francois d'Youville, who proved to be an unfaithful husband and an unscrupulous character, who accrued an enormous debt before leaving Marguerite a widow at age 29. By then, Marguerite had given birth to six children, of whom only two reached adulthood.

True to her independent, resourceful spirit, Marguerite soon opened a small store, which paid off dead husband's debts, sustained her own family, and helped the needy. In 1737, opening her home and a new way of life to "street girls" and other needy women, she and three others dedicated themselves to the service of the poor.

Undaunted, they expanded their work. Marguerite offered the dignity of a decent burial to executed criminals, nursed the war-wounded, French and English alike, and risked her life comforting the ill and dying when a smallpox epidemic struck the aboriginal community.

The Sisters of Charity, as they were to be called, were officially recognized by the church in 1745; their rule was approved in 1755. In the meantime, by 1747, Marguerite had made such a positive impression on local authorities that the debt-ridden, crumbling General Hospital of Montreal was entrusted to her. She paid off the debt and enlarged the facility to take in the sick and the destitute.

The sisters made and sold fine clothing, thus making possible the purchase of several farms to support the needy, as well as catechetical instruction of the farmers' children, the rescue of foundlings, retreats for women, and support for impoverished seminarians. And they were not beyond begging door-to-door on behalf of the poorest of the poor.

The life of Marguerite D'Youville stands as a challenge to those in society who close their eyes to the social ills that surround them, claiming a lack of resources or the futility of action in the face of overwhelming need. As the widow of a feckless miscreant, Marguerite may be claimed as a hero by impoverished single parents who find themselves stigmatized by society and blamed for their own misfortune. We celebrate her memory each year on October 17.

66

Mother Elizabeth Ann Bayley Seton

In the Battery Park area of Manhattan, near New York Harbor, sits a historic house. From its colonnaded front porch a contented young married woman, Elizabeth Bayley Seton, could enjoy the bustle of the city. Elizabeth had grown up in New York; she was a toddler when the Revolutionary War broke out. Her father was a surgeon and anatomy professor at what is now Columbia University. Her mother was from a prominent Episcopalian family.

ELIZABETH SETON

Elizabeth's husband William represented his father's ship-merchant business. They had five children: Anna, William, Richard, Catherine and Rebecca. In the midst of this busy life, she found time to work with the poor. She even established a charity, the Society for the Relief of Poor Widows with Small Children.

Then William developed health problems, complicated by worry about business reversals. Seeking a cure for him, the couple traveled to Italy, where he died. Throughout their difficult stay, they had been treated with great kindness by a Catholic family. Elizabeth was deeply touched by this and found herself drawn to Catholicism. She was received into the Catholic faith on her return to the United States. However, this was a time of strong anti-Catholic feeling. As a result of her decision her wealthy family (and many of her friends) cut all ties with her. Now she herself was a poor widow with small children.

Fortunately, a priest invited her to begin a school for girls in Baltimore. This was the first Catholic school in the United States. In 1809, with a small group of other dedicated women, she established a house in Emmitsburg, Maryland. There she formed a religious community, the Sisters of Charity. It was the first congregation founded in the United States. The order grew rapidly, serving hospitals and orphanages, but was most involved with building the Catholic educational system. Elizabeth herself trained teachers and wrote textbooks. She also worked with the poor, nursed the sick and composed hymns and spiritual reflections. She died while still in her forties, having accomplished an extraordinary amount in her short lifetime (1774–1821). She was wife, mother, widow, educator and founder.

Elizabeth is the first native-born American saint. She is buried in the Basilica of St. Elizabeth Ann Seton at Emmitsburg. The Roman Catholic church remembers her each year on January 4.

67

Bishop John Neumann

He held a powerful post, bishop of Philadelphia, when the diocese covered 35,000 square miles. Yet "the gentle bishop," as John Neumann (1811–1860) was called, was a shy and self-effacing man. He wanted only to be a simple missionary priest bringing comfort to his immigrant flock.

John was born in what is now the Czech Republic. As a young seminarian he hoped to come to America, where there were very few priests to assist a surge of immigrants. After several setbacks, he boarded ship on impulse and headed for New York. He had no papers and was not even ordained yet.

Fortunately, the local bishop welcomed him. He was first assigned to the mission parishes in the Buffalo area. Though few of his immigrant parishioners spoke his native language, Czech, he had studied German, English and French as a schoolboy. Eventually he learned Gaelic, Spanish and Italian. This made it possible for people to receive the sacrament of reconciliation in their own language. Many of his parishioners hadn't had the opportunity to do this for many years.

Since the parishes of this area were rural and spread far apart, he traveled constantly. As a safeguard against the isolation of this work he joined the Redemptorist Order. Soon he was the head of all the Redemptorists in the United States. Then the bishop of Philadelphia recommended John as his successor. To John's chagrin, he was appointed.

As bishop, John built churches and schools, instituted a religious education program for children, and prepared English and German catechisms that remained in use long after he died. He also continued to travel throughout the diocese, which at that time included Delaware, eastern Pennsylvania and part of New Jersey, visiting each parish and mission every two years. Not everyone appreciated this. He was criticized for not having ceremonial manners and for appearing in public in old patched clothes instead of the rich garb a bishop was expected to wear.

However, the people of his diocese loved him for his willingness to reach out to them. When he died suddenly at the age of 48, they lined the streets of Baltimore by the thousands to say goodby to him.

His body is buried at St. Peter, the Redemptorist church in Baltimore. The Roman Catholic church remembers Bishop Neumann each year on January 5.

68

Mother Katharine Drexel

She gave her millions as cheerfully as she devoted her life," said Time magazine when Mother Katharine Drexel died in 1955 at the age of 96. Born into a world of wealth in 1858, she left behind a world made the richer by her presence.

Young Kate Drexel was a genuine heiress. Her grandfather had founded an international banking firm. She grew up with all the trappings of wealth — a Philadelphia townhome, private tutors, extensive vacations and an elegant summer home. She took it all in stride, never wanting to be the center of attention.

Perhaps her gentle spirit was a result of the way she had been raised. Katharine's parents made generous donations to charity, and her mother assisted the poor in all kinds of ways. The couple carefully passed along these values to their children. When Kate was 26, both her parents became ill and died. She inherited a substantial fortune.

By this time in her life, Katharine had already discovered the concern that would become her lifelong passion. On a family trip to the state of Washington, she had seen Native Americans living in grinding poverty with little or no educational opportunity. This had grieved her so much that on a subsequent trip to Europe, she begged Pope Leo XIII to send missionaries to America to work on reservations. To her shock, he responded, "My child, why don't you become a missionary yourself?"

Eventually, she did just that. Gathering a community of 13 like-minded women around her, she founded the Sisters of the Blessed Sacrament. Their special concern was service to Native and African Americans.

They set to work, taking as their first project a school for Pueblo Indians in Santa Fe, New Mexico. Eventually they founded and staffed schools in 16 states, including one in New Orleans that grew into Xavier University. Xavier was founded specifically to serve African American students, who were refused admission to other colleges in the area because of segregation.

The money Mother Katharine had inherited was used for construction and maintenance of all these foundations. Over the course of her life, she funneled twenty million dollars into service of the poor. On October 1, 2000, she was canonized by Pope John Paul II. Mother Katharine is remembered each year on March 3. Her shrine is located in Bensalem, Pennsylvania.

69

Blessed Junipero Serra

Junipero Serra (1713–1784) played a significant part in the history of the United States, Canada and the church itself. He was born on the island of Majorca off the coast of Spain. He joined the Franciscans in Palma, Majorca, at the age of 16. After ordination he became a philosophy professor of some stature at the university there. However, he felt drawn to the work of the Franciscan missions in Mexico.

Padre Serra sailed for the Americas at the age of 35. After six months at the university in Mexico City, he volunteered to serve at the remote mountain missions of Sierra Gorda. He was the first missionary there to learn Otomi, the local language. During his eight-year stay he saw to the building of several churches, which are still in use. During this time he defended Native American property rights against encroachment by Europeans.

When Serra was 55 years old, the Spanish decided to explore Alta California (now the state of California). Though not in the best of health, he traveled along. He described the region as "a veritable paradise." He wanted to establish a string of missions, each a day's walk from the last, all the way up the Pacific coast. Mission San Diego was the first. Each mission became a trading center and then a city. Ultimately 21 missions were established along El Camino Real. Padre Serra founded nine of them. Though his health continued to deteriorate, Serra traveled constantly between the missions. He died at age 70. He had traveled an estimated 24,000 miles during his lifetime.

Sadly from today's perspective, Serra and the other missioners worked closely with the government of Spain. It wanted the Indian lands for Spanish settlers seeking to make their fortunes in the new territories. The soldiers burned the crops and villages of the Native Americans, who then had no choice but to move to the local mission and begin a totally new way of life. In some cases, whole tribes were wiped out by the shock of these sudden changes in lifestyle.

There has thus been some controversy attending the beatification of Junipero Serra in 1988. Because of the harsh treatment received by Native Americans from the military forces of Spain and even from the missionaries, many historians and Native American groups oppose his canonization. He is buried at San Carlos Borromeo Mission in Carmel, California.

Copyright © 2001 Archdiocese of Chicago: Liturgy Training Publications, 1800 North Hermitage Avenue, Chicago IL 60622-1101; 1-800-933-1800; www.ltp.org. Text by Mary Ellen Hynes. Art by Steve Erspamer, SM. All rights reserved. Used with permission.

70

Martyrs Isaac Jogues, John de Brebeuf and Companions

Among the the first French to come to the United States when Europeans explored and conquered the Americas were eight Jesuits who now share the title of "the North American Martyrs." Even before they arrived, tension had begun to build between the Native American population and the French. The Iroquois had been attacked by Samuel Champlain in 1609, and since then the French had proceeded to take the best hunting grounds away from the native people.

ISAAC AND COMPANIONS

Into this tense setting came Jesuits, hoping to preach the gospel. They built a mission at Sainte Marie, consisting of a hospital, fort and cemetery. They worked mostly with the Hurons, who were considered enemies by the Iroquois.

In 1642 lay brother René Goupil (1606–1642) and Father Isaac Jogues (1607–

1646) were captured by a party of Mohawk Iroquois. Goupil was killed; Jogues was held captive for a year before being ransomed. Traveling home to France, he gathered his strength. In 1644 he returned, hoping to help work out a peace treaty between the Hurons and the Iroquois. When it was completed, he was captured by a war party and killed, along with lay missioner John LaLande.

The Iroquois began attacking Huron villages. As they massed at the settlement of St. Joseph in 1648, Father Anthony Daniel went out to meet them alone. He hoped that the Hurons would be spared because of his death. In 1649, Father John de Brebeuf and Gabriel Lalemant were tortured and killed. Lalemant had arrived at the mission only a few weeks earlier. De Brebeuf, the leader of the team, had worked there for 24 years. He had composed catechisms and a dictionary in the Huron language.

Later that year, Father Charles Garnier was shot down attempting to minister to the people of his village during an attack by the Iroquois. Shortly after that, Father Noel Chabanel was killed by a Huron Christian who was angry about the changes brought by the Europeans.

These eight were the first Christian martyrs of the North American continent. Their shrines at Auriesville, New York, and Midland, Ontario, are visited by many pilgrims each year. They are remembered on October 19.

71

Mother Frances Xavier Cabrini

"The whole world is not big enough for me," remarked the small woman. The travels of Frances Xavier Cabrini (1850–1917) took her from Italy to the United States, and across the states from New Jersey to Washington, from Illinois to Lousiana.

Frances was the youngest child in a large family in Italy. She had always dreamed of spreading the gospel in China, as her patron saint Francis Xavier had done. After training as a teacher, she applied to a convent, but was refused entrance. She worked with orphans for a few years and then decided to begin a community of missionary sisters. Soon an abandoned friary became the new home of the Missionary Sisters of the Sacred Heart.

Instead of heading east, soon the sisters headed west — to America. Of the tens of thousands of newly arrived Italian immigrants in New York City at the end of the nineteenth century, very few had any formal religious education and work kept many from Mass. Archbishop Corrigan invited Frances to bring some of her missionaries to New York. But when they arrived, circumstances had caused the archbishop to change his plans, and he suggested that the sisters return to Italy on the next boat.

Frances had other plans. Known for her shrewd handling of money, she always trusted that God would provide the materials goods that her sisters would need to do their work. And she was right. By the time she died, Frances Xavier Cabrini had begun 67 schools, orphanages and hospitals. These were spread across the United States, Central and South America, Italy, France and England.

It is recorded that she traversed the ocean 30 times — in the days before airplanes. And after she died, her sisters fulfilled her original dream and went on mission to China.

Mother Cabrini was the first U.S. citizen to be canonized a saint. She is the patron saint of immigrants and is remembered each year on November 13.

Pioneer Rose Philippine Duchesne

In 1918 the Missouri Historical Society named Sister Rose Philippine Duchesne the greatest of the state's pioneer women. Although her life was a series of extraordinary adventures, those who met her were most struck by her spirit of quiet reflection.

Philippine (as she was known) was born in Grenoble in France. She grew up during the turbulent times prior to the French Revolution. Her father, a lawyer, was also an outspoken politician who believed that the monarchy should be overthrown. Her mother was a person of faith in a time when that was not fashionable. Philippine, who was strongly influenced by her, joined a convent. Shortly afterward, though, the Revolution began, and all convents and monasteries were disbanded. Philippine spent the next ten years teaching neglected children and caring for the sick.

When the Reign of Terror ended and a spirit of greater religious tolerance emerged, she and four other nuns from her convent joined a new religious order, the Society of the Sacred Heart. Thus she came to know Mother Madeleine Sophie Barat, who would herself become canonized.

Philippine longed to work with Native Americans. At the age of 49 she was sent to the United States as superior of a small group of sisters. They had been invited to assist the archbishop of St. Louis with religious instruction. In the village of St. Charles, Missouri she founded a convent in a small log cabin and began a school for the daughters of pioneer settlers. It was the first free school west of the Mississippi. During the next few years, she also founded schools in Mississippi and Louisiana. She and her sisters suffered all kinds of hardships, from forest fires and epidemics to hunger. In her work with settlers, she fought prejudice against African Americans.

In 1840, at the age of 71, she accompanied a group of sisters opening a mission for Potawatomi Indians at what is now Sugar Creek, Missouri. At last her vision of serving among Native Americans had been realized.

PHIL IPPI NE

Too frail to teach, she prayed while the other sisters worked with the children. The Potawatomi described her as "the woman who prays always." After only a year at the mission, she became ill. At the age of 83 she died at St. Charles, where she is buried.

Rose Philippine Duchesne was canonized in 1988. We remember her each year on November 18.

Copyright © 2001 Archdiocese of Chicago: Liturgy Training Publications, 1800 North Hermitage Avenue, Chicago IL 60622-1101; 1-800-933-1800; www.ltp.org. Text by Mary Ellen Hynes. Art by Steve Erspamer, SM. All rights reserved. Used with permission.

73

Whose House is This?

Whose house is the church building, God's or ours?

The answer is yes! Both! Our church is God's house *because* it is the house of the body of Christ, the church. We cannot contain God. We cannot imprison God in some

Notre Dame, Ronchamps (20th century)

structure made of human hands. But when we who are made holy by baptism, confirmation and eucharist gather together, then God chooses to live here in this place, among us. When we who are God's church gather together, with our bishop (or his delegate, the priest) and the deacon, around our book (on its stand), at our font (and its water), and especially around the Lord's altar (which is a dining table set in the shadow of the cross), God choses to dwell here, too.

The God who wove the night time sky and buttoned it with stars, the God for whom the Rocky Mountains are naught but a bit of mud squished between divine toes, and for whom the oceans are but puddles — this God does not need a temple. But the people whom this God loves from before time began do need a place to gather, and to remember in sacred rites that the church is made of flesh and blood before it is made of brick and board. Our church building is that place! So it should be simply beautiful, and we should care lovingly for it. It isn't any old meeting hall. It isn't any old living room. It isn't a museum or a classroom, either. It is a holy place, a holy land right here in our neighborhood where the body of Christ is joined, where the voice of Christ rings out, where the sacrifice of Christ is offered and shared.

It is good to show reverence in and to the church building. But reverence is not ignoring one's neighbor as a distraction. Reverence is the wonder that we experience and the love that we show when we realize that each one of those here gathered around the Lord's altar is a living stone that builds a spiritual house, and it is here that God truly lives among us.

S. Ambrogio, Milan (late 11th–12th century)

74

Q&A: A Bigger Font

Many new or renovated churches have large baptismal fonts that look like pools. Why?

In our tradition, water brings to mind the chaos before creation, the great flood, the parted Red Sea, the water that flowed from the rock in the desert, Christ's baptism in the Jordan. These images provide the background for our use of water, particularly in baptism, and should influence the design of the fonts in which water is stored.

When the sacramental rites were revised after the Second Vatican Council (1962–1965), the general introduction to the baptismal rites noted that baptism could be celebrated either by immersion or by pouring water over the head of a candidate (*Christian Initiation,* General Introduction, 22). In order to allow an adult to be baptized by immersion, new and renovated churches often have baptismal fonts which are small pools into which an adult can walk and in which the adult can kneel for the sacramental washing.

In Romans 6:3–5, Saint Paul wrote that through baptism we are buried with Christ, and entering a large font for baptism by immersion can evoke the image of a entering a tomb only to rise again with the risen Lord. For this reason, one ancient image of the baptismal font is that of the "tomb." Because Jesus speaks about being "born of water and the Spirit" (John 3:5), another ancient image of the font is that of the "womb." In contrast, many fonts of the last few centuries look like bird baths!

Newer baptismal fonts are actually a return to a more ancient form of the baptism pool. Revised liturgical books even

mention that such fonts might include flowing water, reminding us of Christ's statement that "from him shall flow rivers of living water" (John 7:38). Rather than being a novelty, large pool-like fonts and celebrating baptism by immersion encourage us to return to a symbolically richer form of celebrating the sacrament of rebirth and resurrection, and help us recall the many ways that water refreshes, cleanses, quenches, and renews us during each day of our lives.

Baptism by immersion has been always been permitted in the western church, but various historical influences led to baptism by pouring being the standard method until the reforms of Vatican II. Eastern Christian churches have, in general, preserved the custom of celebrating baptism by immersion over the centuries. In fact, the word "baptism" is derived from the Greek word for "immersion." For this and other reasons, the revised baptismal rites recommend that the western church also use immersion when possible since it is "more suitable as a symbol of participation in the death and resurrection of Christ."

75

Q&A: The Tabernacle

What is church law about the place for the tabernacle?

In 1969 the *General Instruction of the Roman Missal* gave "encouragement" to a separate chapel for the tabernacle (#276) for parish churches. The 1973 Vatican document, *Holy Communion and Worship of the Eucharist Outside of Mass,* states that honoring the Lord, present in the sacrament, "will be achieved more easily if the [eucharistic] chapel is separate from the body of the church" (#9). Then, the 1984 *Ceremonial of Bishops* made an even stronger statement in the case of a cathedral. Paragraph 49 explicitly recommends that "in accordance with a very ancient tradition" the tabernacle "should be located in a chapel separate from the main body of the church," and even mandates that if (in some church) "there is a tabernacle on the altar at which the bishop is to celebrate, the blessed sacrament should be transferred to another fitting place."

Since the 1983 *Code of Canon Law* applies equally to large cathedrals and small convent chapels, it says relatively little about the location of the tabernacle, mentioning only in very general terms that it should "placed in a part of the church that is prominent, conspicuous, beautifully decorated, and suitable for prayer." It specifically leaves details to the liturgical books, so this canon must be interpreted in light of the other books which speak about the tabernacle in greater detail. In fact, a list of specific changes to earlier published rubrics mandated by the 1983 *Code of Canon Law* made no changes to the General Instruction's guidelines for the tabernacle or to those found in the 1973 document on eucharistic worship outside of Mass, even though other paragraphs in the same documents were explicitly modified.

The revised 2000 *General Instruction of the Roman Missal* no longer encourages the use of a separate chapel for the tabernacle, but instead lists the separate chapel as one of two options, the other option being having the tabernacle in the sanctuary (but not on the altar that is used to celebrate Mass). The fact that the separate chapel is listed as the second of the two options does not imply that somewhere it is the lesser choice. The 1973 document mentioned above, *Holy Communion and the Worship of the Eucharist outside of Mass,* has not been contravened by the revised General Instruction, so the reasons that it presents in promoting a separate chapel still stand. The revised General Instruction does introduce a new idea: It explicitly gives the local bishop authority to decide the best place for the tabernacle in the churches and chapels of the diocese.

Suggested Schedule Sunday by Sunday

This list offers one possible plan or outline for an entire year's worth of articles. It begins with the First Sunday of Advent (1) and ends with Christ the King Sunday (52). The final order will vary depending on the calendar cycle for a particular year. The articles lilsted in italics are not time-specific and may be used on other dates, or even repeated in the course of the year, as needed.

1. *The Church Prays with Attention*
2. *Before You Said Amen*
3. *Gift Giving*
4. *When Was Jesus Born?*
5. *Giving a Blessing*
6. *Mother Seton, Bishop Neumann*
       or *Blessed André*
7. *Saint Marguerite Bourgeoys*
8. *Smudged with Ashes* or *Mother Drexel*
9. *Lent at Home* or *To Eat or Not to Eat*
10. *Which Three Days* or *Spiritual Carrots*
11. *Pilgrims, Palms, Processions*
       or *Spiritual Direction*
12. *Matthew's Passion, Mark Struggled, Jews
       and Christians Together*
       or *Experiencing Hunger*
13. *The Guilt of Us All, A Way to Understand
       John* or *Fasting Together*
14. *Stand Watch* or *On Mealtime as Prayer*
15. *Feasting at Easter* or *Water*
16. *Bread* or *Mass Begins at Home*
17. *Wine* or *Keeping Sunday*
18. *Wood, Walking Meditation*
       or *Blessed Kateri*
19. *Wax* or *More on Walking Meditation*
20. *Incense, Holy Days in History*
       or *Day or Date?*
21. *Oil* or *Walk the Walk*
22. *Chrism* or *Q&A: My Own Cup?*
23. *Keeping Silence*
24. *Do We Think We Change God's Mind?*
25. *Before You Said Amen*
26. *The Church Prayers with Attention*
27. *What Gets Changed?*
28. *A Habit of the Catholic Heart*
29. *Are We Ready for This Prayer?*

30. *Blessed Junipero Serra* or *Blessed Kateri*
31. *The Whole Church Celebrates*
32. *Q&A: Always a Mass?*
33. *Preparing Yourselves for Marriage*
34. *Here Comes the Bride*
       or *Q&A: Is It the Bride's March*
35. *Wedding Traditions*
36. *Wedding Music*
37. *The Cantor at Weddings*
38. *Preparing Your Wedding Liturgy*
39. *Wedding Customs*
40. *Saint Marguerite D'Youville*
41. *Martyrs Isaac Jogues, John de Brebeuf
       and Companions*
42. *Halloween and All Saints*
43. Remembering the Dead
44. *Q&A: A Bigger Font*
45. *Whose House Is This*
46. *Mother Cabrini*
47. *Pioneer Rose Philippine Duchesne*
48. *Q&A: Godparents*
49. *Q&A: Confirmation Names*
50. *Whose House Is This?*
51. *Q&A: The Tabernacle*
52. *Until the Fat Lady Sings*
       or *Remembering the Dead*

Record of Use Chart

Article	For Whom/Publication	Date Used
Are We Ready for This Prayer?		
Before You Said Amen		
Blessed Brother André		
Blessed Junipero Serra		
Blessed Kateri Tekakwitha		
Bishop John Neumann		
Bread		
Chrism		
The Church Prays With Attention		
Day or Date?		
Do We Think That We Change God's Mind		
Experiencing Hunger		
Fasting Together		
Feasting at Easter		
Gift Giving		
Giving a Blessing		
The Guilt of Us All		
A Habit of the Catholic Heart		
Halloween and All Saints		
Here Comes the Bride		
Holy Days in History		
Incense		
Jews and Christian Together		
Keeping Silence		
Keeping Sunday		
Lent at Home		
Mark Struggled for an "Israel of the Nations"		
Martyrs Isaac Jogues, John de Brebeuf		
Mass Begins at Home		
Matthew's Passion in Context		
More on Walking Meditation		
Mother Elizabeth Ann Bayley Seton		
Mother Frances Xavier Cabrini		
Mother Katharine Drexel		
Oil		

Article	For Whom/Publication	Date Used
On Mealtime Prayer		
Pilgrims, Palms, Processions		
Pioneer Rose Philippine Duchesne		
Preparing Your Wedding Liturgy		
Preparing Yourselves to Celebrate Marriage		
Q&A: Always a Mass?		
Q&A: A Bigger Font		
Q&A: Less Can Be More		
Q&A: Confirmation Names		
Q&A: Godparents		
Q&A: My Own Cup?		
Q&A: The Tabernacle		
Q&A: Who Marches Up the Aisle?		
Remembering the Dead		
Saint Marguerite Bourgeoys		
Saint Marguerite D'Youville		
Smudged with Ashes		
Spiritual Carrots		
Spiritual Direction		
Stand Watch		
Sunday Mass Times		
To Eat or Not to Eat		
Until the Fat Lady Sings		
Walk the Walk		
Walking Meditation		
Water		
Wax		
A Way to Understand John		
Wedding Customs		
Wedding Music		
Wedding Traditions		
What Gets Changed?		
When Was Jesus Born?		
Which Three Days		
The Whole Church Celebrates		
Whose House Is This?		
Wine		
Wood		

CLIP NOTES FOR CHURCH BULLETINS • CD-ROM INFORMATION

HOW TO USE The CD on the inside back cover contains word processing files for both the text and artwork printed in this book. These files can be read and printed by either MS-DOS/IBM-PCs or MACINTOSH computers. If you wish to reproduce pages exactly as they look in the book, you may use the Acrobat Portable Document Files (PDFs) available in the PDF subdirectory. Installers for Adobe Acrobat Reader, the program needed to read and print these files, are included on the CD in the Acrobat subdirectory.

To explore this disk, insert the CD in your computer's CD-ROM drive. Change to the CD-ROM drive and to the subdirectory named for the word processing program you use. There you will find text files named for the article numbers in this book. The artwork can be found in the ART subdirectory.

MS-DOS/IBM-PC compatible formats are WordPerfect, Microsoft Publisher and Microsoft Word. If you are using any of these programs, or a later version, you may import or merge the text file you want into your own document. (MS Publisher requires that you copy files to your fixed disk drive and remove their read-only attributes before opening.) If you are using a different program, you will need to import a desired file from WordPerfect or Word.

MACINTOSH formats included on the CD are WordPerfect, Microsoft Word and Claris Works. Import these files directly into your software (if you are using one of these programs) or convert into your software format if you are using a different program.

ARTWORK is available as TIF files. Each file (or piece of art) is named for its article number in this book. Please refer to article numbers for the file names you want.

LICENSE AND LIMITED WARRANTY As with the printed pages of this book, this CD-ROM is licensed for exclusive use by the original purchaser. Liturgy Training Publications warrants that the CD-ROM is free from defect in material and workmanship for a period of thirty days from the date of purchase. Defective CDs must be returned to LTP within this warranty period in order to be replaced at no charge. This program is provided "AS IS" and Liturgy Training Publications is in no way liable or responsible for any problems that may arise from its use. This statement shall be construed, interpreted and governed by the laws of the State of Illinois.

COPYRIGHT Except for adaptations of format, size and type fonts, no part of the text or artwork provided on the CD may be changed, deleted or altered in any fashion without the permission of Liturgy Training Publications. The copyright notice as found on each page must appear with each use.

FOR ASSISTANCE, CALL TECHNICAL SUPPORT AT 1-773-486-8970 x256.